A GUIDE FOR MARRIED MEN

STOP LYING

How the Lies You Tell Are Destroying the Life You Want to Keep

HASANI PETTIFORD

BASED ON OVER A DECADE OF COACHING WORK WITH MORE THAN ONE THOUSAND MEN

Published by Couples Academy Publishing

www.couplesacademy.org

Email: info@couplesacademy.org

First Edition

Printed in the United States of America

For information about bulk purchases,
training sessions, or speaking engagements, contact:

www.couplesacademy.org | **hasani@couplesacademy.org** |
+1-678-200-8996

ALSO BY HASANI PETTIFORD

- Wealth Builders: An Economic Program For African American Youth
- Black Thighs, Black Guys & Bedroom Lies
- Pimpin' From The Pulpit To The Pews
- The 12 Habits of Successful People
- The 12 Habits of Wealthy People
- The 12 Habits of Healthy People
- The 12 Habits of Effective Leaders
- Why We Hate Black Women and
- Why We Should Love Them
- 7 Days of Extraordinary Sex
- 101 Ways To Love My Wife
- 101 Ways To Love My Husband
- The Audacity of Marriage: 10 Principles For Life-long Partnership
- The 100 Day Husbands Challenge
- Love Challenge
- Study Your Wife: A Husband's Guide To Unlocking Deeper Intimacy and Connection
- SKIN PLEASURE: 12 Pathways to Erotic Intelligence

TABLE OF CONTENTS

THE STOP LYING WORKBOOK

Exercises, Reflections, and a 30-Day Honesty Challenge

FOREWORD

A NOTE FROM THE COACH

I have sat across from over a thousand men. Men in suits. Men in work boots. Men with $40,000 watches and men who couldn't make rent. Men who coached Little League on Saturdays and slept in their cars on Wednesdays. Men with twenty years of marriage behind them and men who were still in the honeymoon phase when everything started to fall apart.

They came to me for different reasons. Marriages on the edge. Affairs that had been discovered. Patterns of behavior they couldn't explain. Lives that looked fine from the outside and felt like a slow collapse from the inside. But almost every single one of them had one thing in common. They were lying.

Not just to their wives. Not just to their families. They were lying to themselves — and had been for so long, they had stopped being able to tell the difference between the truth and the story they'd been telling.

I want to be clear about something before you read another word of this book. I am not writing this to shame you. I am not writing this to call you a monster. I have spent enough time in rooms with real men to know that the ones who lie the most are rarely the ones who feel the least — they are often the ones who feel the most and have absolutely no idea what to do with it.

Shame built the lies. More shame will not tear them down. But I am also not writing this to coddle you. If that is what you are looking for, there are other books. This is not that book.

This book is going to tell you the truth — about why you lie, what it is costing you, what it is doing to the people you claim to love, and exactly what it takes to stop. Not slow down. Not manage. Stop.

> ***"The truth will set you free. But first, it will make you deeply uncomfortable." — a phrase I have said in coaching rooms more times than I can count.***

Over the years, working with men in crisis and men who had not yet hit crisis but were heading there at full speed, I began to see patterns so consistent they felt like a blueprint. The same lies. The same fears underneath the lies. The same moment of reckoning when a man finally stopped running from himself.

That blueprint is this book. I am writing from what I have witnessed, not from what I have lived. My seat has been the chair across the table — the one where you have to watch a man wrestle with whether he is willing to become someone different. I have watched men choose truth and rebuild things I did not think could be rebuilt. I have watched men choose to keep lying and lose everything they said they were lying to protect.

The difference between those two groups was never intelligence, or willpower, or how badly things had gotten. The difference was a decision — a single, bone-deep decision to stop living in two worlds.

Who this book is for

This book is for the man who is actively cheating and knows it needs to stop but does not know how to stop without blowing up his life. It is for the man who has been caught and is now trying to figure out if there is anything left to save — and who he is going to be going forward.

It is for the man who has never cheated but lies about money, about where he has been, about what he feels, about who he really is — the man who is slowly building a wall between himself and his wife one small deception at a time.

It is for the man who looks at himself in the mirror and knows, without anyone telling him, that he is not the man he said he would be.

You do not have to have had an affair to need this book. You just have to be willing to be honest about the fact that you have not been honest.

What this book will not do

This book will not save your marriage. That is not its job.

What happens to your marriage depends on too many variables for any book to promise you an outcome. What I can tell you is this: no marriage, no family, no relationship of any real depth survives if you do not first fix what is broken inside you. You are the variable.

You are the one holding the match.

The goal of this book is not to make your wife trust you again. The goal is to make you a man who is worth trusting. Those are related but they are not the same thing. One is about your marriage.

The other is about your character. And your character will outlast any relationship, any crisis, any season of your life.

Start there. Start with the man in the mirror. If you do, everything else has a fighting chance.

How to read this book

Read it straight through the first time. Do not skip ahead to the chapter that sounds most relevant to you. The book is built in sequence — each part of the journey depends on what came before it.

At the back, you will find the Stop Lying Workbook. It is designed to be used after you have read the main text, or chapter by chapter as you go. Either way, do not skip it. The reading will show you the map. The workbook is where you actually walk the road.

One more thing. There are moments in this book where I will reference scripture — not to preach at you, not to tell you what to believe, but because some of what was written thousands of years ago about men, truth, and the cost of deception is still the most precise language available for what I am trying to say. Take it or leave it. The point underneath it will hold either way.

Now. Let's get to work.

— The Coach

From the desk of someone who has watched a thousand men choose — and knows it is always, always still a choice.

INTRODUCTION

BEFORE WE BEGIN

This book almost did not get written. Not because the subject matter was unclear. Not because there was any shortage of material. After more than a decade of sitting with men in the most honest conversations they had probably ever had — conversations about deception, about the double lives they were running, about the marriages they were destroying one lie at a time — I had more material than I could ever put into a single volume. The reason this book almost did not get written is simpler and more uncomfortable than that. I was not sure men would read it.

Not because men do not read. Not because the subject does not affect them. Because the particular man this book is written for — the man who is lying to his wife, who is hiding something significant, who has built a carefully managed version of his life that does not match the reality he is actually living — that man has spent years developing a highly sophisticated set of skills for avoiding exactly this kind of direct confrontation with himself. He has become expert at changing the subject, finding the exit, concluding that this particular resource does not quite apply to his particular situation, which is, of course, more complicated than anyone on the outside could understand.

I wrote it anyway. Because I have watched what happens to men who never have this confrontation. And I have watched what happens to men who finally do. And the difference between those two outcomes is not small. It is not a matter of degree. It is the difference between a life that is actually lived and a life that is managed from behind glass — visible to everyone, accessible to no one, including the man living it.

Let me tell you what I see from where I sit.

I see men who are, by most external measures, successful. They provide. They show up. They coach the teams and attend the recitals and sit in the front rows of the school plays. They say the right things at the right moments. They have learned, with impressive precision, how to present the life of a good man without fully inhabiting it. And underneath all of that — underneath the performance, underneath the competence, underneath the carefully constructed image of the husband and father and solid citizen — there is a man who is exhausted. Not from the work. From the weight of what he is carrying that nobody knows about.

The lying is that weight. Not always an affair — though often enough. Sometimes it is financial deception, the hiding of debt or addiction or catastrophic decisions made without her knowledge. Sometimes it is emotional absence disguised as busyness, the slow withdrawal of a man who stopped being honest about his interior life so gradually that neither he nor his wife can identify exactly when the distance became permanent.

Sometimes it is the accumulation of a thousand small managed moments — questions deflected, feelings denied, truths softened until they became something else entirely. Whatever form it takes, the lying is always the weight. And the weight is always costing more than the man carrying it is willing to admit.

I wrote this book for that man. The one who is tired of carrying it even if he has not yet said so out loud. The one who picked this up because something in the title felt uncomfortably accurate. The one who is reading these words right now with a specific and personal kind of recognition that he is hoping I will not push too hard on. I am going to push on it. That is what this book is for.

Here is what I know after more than a decade of this work, after sitting with men in their worst moments and their most honest ones, after watching some of them rebuild what I did not think could be rebuilt and watching others lose everything they claimed they were trying to protect.

The lying is never really about the thing being lied about. It is never, at the deepest level, about the affair or the money or the addiction or the hollow performance of a marriage that stopped being real years ago. Those are the contents of the lie. The lie itself — the pattern, the habit, the reflex — is about something older and more fundamental. It is about a man who learned, somewhere along the way, that the true version of himself was not safe to show. That honesty had consequences he was not willing to absorb. That managing other people's perception of him was more survivable than letting them see him clearly.

That lesson was probably learned before this marriage. Before this woman. Before any of the specific circumstances that are currently making your life complicated. It was likely learned in childhood, in the particular atmosphere of the home you grew up in, in the messages — spoken and unspoken — about what men do with what they feel and what they hide and what they perform. And it has been running, below the level of conscious decision, ever since. Governing your choices without your awareness. Building structures you did not entirely intend and now do not entirely know how to dismantle.

This book is about dismantling them. Not quickly. Not painlessly. But completely, and in a way that actually holds. I want to be precise about what this book is and what it is not, because clarity at the beginning saves confusion later.

This is not a book about saving your marriage. I understand that may be what you most want — it may be the reason you picked this up, the hope that somewhere in these pages is the formula that keeps the family together and avoids the explosion and produces the outcome you can live with. I am not going to tell you that hope is wrong. What I am going to tell you is that it is the wrong starting point. A marriage saved by a man who has not genuinely changed is not saved. It is deferred. The same patterns, the same habits, the same divisions between the interior life and the exterior performance — they do not disappear because a crisis was narrowly avoided. They go underground and wait.

This is a book about you. About the man you have become and the man you are capable of being and the distance between those two things, and what it actually takes to close it. The marriage, if it survives, will survive as a consequence of that work. But the work itself is personal.

It is about your character, your integrity, your relationship with the truth, your capacity to be fully known by another human being without flinching. Those things will outlast this marriage, whatever happens to it. They will determine the quality of every relationship you ever have and the kind of man your children grow up knowing and the kind of person you are able to look at in the mirror without calculation.

Start there. The rest follows or it does not, but it follows from that or it does not follow at all. A word about how this book is structured, because the structure is intentional and the sequence matters.

The first three chapters build the foundation of understanding — what lying actually is, how it works in the brain, and how it compounds over time into something far larger and more damaging than any single deception. These chapters ask you to see the pattern clearly before we start tracing it to its source.

The next three chapters go deeper — into the identity questions, the real motivations, and the origins of the habit in your personal history. This is the section most men find most uncomfortable, because it requires sitting with things they have worked very hard not to look at directly.

Chapters seven and eight are the cost chapters — a full and unflinching accounting of what the lying is already extracting from your life and what the moment of reckoning looks like when it arrives. These chapters are not designed to shame you. They are designed to make the status quo feel exactly as untenable as it actually is.

The final four chapters are the turn. The decision, the practical steps, the accountability structures, and the vision of the man waiting on the other side of this work. This is the section where the book stops describing the problem and starts building the solution.

At the back, you will find the Stop Lying Workbook — exercises, reflections, a trigger map, a truth declaration, and a thirty-day honesty challenge. Read the book first. Then work through it. The reading gives you the map. The workbook is where you walk the road.

One more thing before Chapter One begins, and it may be the most important thing I say in this entire book.

You are not beyond this. I do not care how long the lying has been running, how complex the web has become, how much damage has already been done, or how convinced you are that you are somehow a special case for whom the ordinary rules of human change do not apply. You are not a special case. You are a man with a deeply ingrained pattern of behavior that was learned under specific conditions and has been reinforced through years of repetition.

That pattern can be unlearned. The brain can be rewired. The habit can be broken. I have watched it happen in men who were further gone than you are right now, men who had done more damage and carried more shame and built more elaborate structures of deception than anything you are currently managing.

They changed. Not because they were exceptional. Because they decided to. Because they stopped finding reasons why their situation was too complicated for honesty and started asking what honesty would actually require of them, specifically, in their specific life, and then did that thing.

That is the whole path. It is not more complicated than that, and it is not less difficult than it sounds. You picked this book up for a reason. Something in you knows that the way you have been living is not the way you were meant to live. That knowing is not an accident. It is the most honest part of you, the part that never fully made peace with the lie even while you were telling it, trying to get your attention.

It has your attention now. Let us begin.

PART 1

THE TRUTH ABOUT LYING

Understanding what lying is, how it works, and what it has become.

CHAPTER 1

YOU ARE NOT A BAD MAN. YOU ARE A SCARED ONE.

Marcus had been married for eleven years when he first sat down across from me. He was the kind of man you would never look at twice in a grocery store — average height, quiet eyes, the kind of handshake that tells you a person was raised right. He coached his son's baseball team. He called his mother every Sunday. He had a good job, a nice house, and a wife who, by every account, loved him deeply. He had also been lying to her for most of their marriage.

Not about everything. Not in the cartoon way people imagine when they hear the word liar. He had not constructed some elaborate false identity or faked a career or hidden a secret family across town. His lies were quieter than that, and in many ways more damaging for their quietness. He lied about where he had been. He lied about money he had spent. He lied about a relationship with a woman from work that had started as friendship and slowly, over the course of two years, become something else. He lied by saying "I'm fine" every time he was not. He lied by nodding when she talked about the future, all while carrying a present he had not told her about.

When I asked Marcus why he lied, he looked at the floor for a long time. Then he said something I have heard in some version from nearly every man I have ever worked with.

"I don't know. I just couldn't tell her the truth. I couldn't stand the way she would look at me."

That right there. That is not evil. That is fear. And fear, not wickedness, is what sits at the center of almost every lie a married man tells.

I want you to sit with that for a moment, because I know what some of you are thinking. You are thinking that calling it fear is just another way of letting yourself off the hook. You have probably heard it before — men talking about their pain as an explanation for their behavior, using their wounds as a reason why their wives should extend them more grace. That is not what I am doing here, and if that is where your mind went, I need you to course-correct right now.

Understanding that fear drives your lying is not an excuse. It is a diagnosis. And you cannot treat something you refuse to accurately name. So we are going to name it. We are going to name it clearly and without flinching, because the first lie most men tell is the one they tell themselves about why they lie.

They say: I did it to protect her.

They say: I didn't want to hurt her.

They say: It's complicated, you don't understand our marriage.

And underneath all of those explanations, if you press long enough and hard enough and the man in the chair finally gets tired of performing, what you find is something much simpler and much more honest. I was scared. I was scared she would leave. I was scared she would stop seeing me the way I needed her to see me. I was scared that if she knew the real version of what was going on inside me — the doubt, the failure, the wanting, the shame — she would decide I was not worth staying for.

So you lied. Not because you are a monster. Because you are a man who did not know what else to do with the fear.

Research on why men deceive in relationships points consistently to the same cluster of root causes: shame, fear of rejection, the need to protect a self-image that feels fragile, and the desperate desire to avoid conflict. These are not small things. These are the load-bearing walls of a man's psychology, and when they are threatened, the instinct to reach for a lie can feel as automatic as pulling your hand from a hot stove. It happens before you even consciously decide to do it. The story is out of your mouth before the truth had a fair chance.

This does not mean you are helpless. It means you are human. But it also means that simply deciding to stop lying is not enough — and any book that tells you it is has not spent enough time in rooms with real men. You cannot white-knuckle your way out of a pattern that lives this deep. You have to understand it first. You have to follow the fear all the way back to where it started, look at it clearly, and then — and only then — make a different choice.

There is a concept in psychology called shame resilience, developed by researcher Brené Brown, and one of its foundational insights is this: shame needs three things to survive: secrecy, silence, and judgment. The moment you bring shame into the light — the moment you name it out loud to another person who responds with empathy rather than contempt — it begins to lose its power over you. Not all at once. Not painlessly. But it begins.

Most men who lie chronically in their marriages are not doing so from a place of power. They are doing so from a place of profound shame. They have something they believe — truly believe, deep in the gut — that if their wife saw it, she would not stay. And that belief, whether or not it is accurate, becomes the engine that runs the entire machine of deception. One lie to cover the shame. Another lie to cover the first lie. A whole architecture of half-truths and misdirections, built not to harm her, but to keep her from seeing the part of you that you are most convinced is unlovable.

I have sat with men who had affairs for three years. Five years. Men who had maintained entire parallel lives — different phones, different email accounts, different versions of who they were — and when you finally got past the defenses and asked them what they were most afraid of, it was never getting caught. It was being truly known. The affair, the lies, the secrecy — all of it was a way of staying close enough to feel loved while staying hidden enough to feel safe. It is an impossible bargain. It always collapses. But it made sense to them in the dark, in the way that only desperate things make sense.

Now let me speak to a different kind of man for a moment — the man who has not had an affair, who would never have an affair, but who lies in smaller and steadier ways. The man who says he's working late when he stayed to avoid going home. The man who says "everything's fine" when he is drowning in anxiety he doesn't know how to explain. The man who nods along to plans he has no intention of following through on because agreement is easier than the conversation that disagreement would require. The man who has been performing "husband" for so long he has forgotten what it would feel like to just be himself.

That is still lying. It is quieter lying. It does not make the front page of a marriage crisis in the same way an affair does. But it does its damage all the same — slowly, steadily, the way water damages a foundation. You do not notice it until the cracks appear. And by the time the cracks appear, you are looking at years of accumulated distance that neither of you can quite explain.

The Proverbs say it plainly: "An honest witness tells the truth, but a false witness tells lies." The word witness matters there. In a marriage, you are a witness to each other's lives. Every time you lie — big or small, to protect yourself or to protect her feelings or simply because the truth felt too heavy to carry into the room — you are bearing false witness to the person who chose to build a life with you. That is not a small thing. That is a fracture at the center of the whole enterprise.

I want to return to Marcus, because his story does not end in the chair across from me looking at the floor. It took Marcus the better part of a year to tell his wife the full truth. Not because he did not want to — once he started working on himself, the desire to come clean became almost unbearable. But because telling the truth, when you have been lying for years, is one of the most terrifying acts a man can perform. You are not just confessing a set of facts. You are dismantling an entire version of yourself and trusting that something real can be built in its place. You are handing someone the precise information she would need to leave you, and asking her to stay anyway.

Marcus's wife did not leave. But that is not the point of telling you his story. Some wives do leave, and sometimes they should. The point is what happened to Marcus. When he finally stopped lying — not just to his wife, but to himself — he described it as the first time in years he could breathe in a room without calculating. Without tracking what he had said to whom. Without that low-grade hum of anxiety that had become so constant he had stopped noticing it was there.

He said: "I didn't even know I had been holding my breath until I finally let it out." That is what truth does. Not just for your marriage. For you. For the man inside all of the performance and the protection and the fear. Truth gives him back his air.

Here is what I need you to take from this chapter before we go any further.

You are not a bad man because you lie. You are a scared man who learned that lying was the safest way to manage the fear. Maybe you learned it as a boy, in a house where the truth had consequences. Maybe you learned it in a culture that told you real men do not show weakness, do not admit failure, do not let anyone see the parts of themselves they cannot control. Maybe you learned it in your marriage, in the early days, when you said something honest and the reaction was so painful that you swore you would never do it again.

However you learned it, it made sense at the time. And it has been costing you ever since. The man who lies to protect himself is always, without exception, destroying the very thing he is trying to protect. You cannot build a real marriage on a managed version of yourself. You cannot be truly loved if the person loving you does not actually know you. You cannot feel safe in a relationship that only exists because you have been careful enough not to let her see who you really are.

The safety you built with your lies is not real safety. It is a cage you made yourself. And you are so used to living in it that you have started to mistake the bars for walls.

In the chapters ahead, we are going to go deeper. We are going to look at the neuroscience of what lying does to a brain over time — how it rewires you, how it makes the next lie easier and the truth feel more dangerous, how a habit this ingrained cannot simply be wished away. We are going to trace the roots of your lying back to where they began, because you did not start this way.

Something taught you that hiding was safer than being seen. We are going to look unflinchingly at what your lying has cost — not in abstract terms, but in the specific, documented damage it does to the people you love and to the man you were capable of becoming. And then we are going to talk about what it actually takes to stop. Not how to lie less. Not how to be more careful. How to stop.

But none of that work is possible until you are willing to begin from an honest place. So I am going to ask you to do something right now, before you turn another page. I am going to ask you to say — out loud if you can, in your own head if that is all you have — one true thing. Not a confession. Not a list of everything you have done. Just one true thing that you have not let yourself say plainly.

It does not have to be pretty. It does not have to be complete. It just has to be real. Because that is where this starts. Not with a plan. Not with a strategy. With one moment of honesty in a life that has had too few of them. You can do that. You are going to have to.

CHAPTER 2

HOW LYING ACTUALLY WORKS IN YOUR BRAIN

There is a moment that almost every man I have coached can describe, even if they have never had a word for it. It is the moment right before the lie. A split second — sometimes less than that — where the truth is available, sitting right there, and then something happens. A switch flips. And what comes out of your mouth instead is the safer version, the managed version, the version that keeps things from getting complicated. And the strange part, the part that should disturb you more than it probably does, is how easy it was. How it barely cost you anything. How it felt almost like breathing.

That feeling is not a coincidence. It is not a sign that you are especially cold or especially skilled at deception. It is neuroscience. Your brain did that. And if you want to understand why you keep lying even when part of you desperately does not want to, you need to understand what your brain has been doing all these years while you were busy looking the other way.

Let's start with what happens the very first time a person tells a significant lie. Researchers using functional MRI — brain imaging technology that tracks activity in real time — have found that the brain lights up in a specific and telling way when a person is being deceptive. The prefrontal cortex, which is responsible for decision-making, problem-solving, and moral reasoning, works harder during a lie than it does during truthful speech. Lying, it turns out, requires more mental effort than telling the truth. It demands that you hold two realities in your head at once — the actual reality and the constructed one — and manage the gap between them without getting caught. That is cognitively expensive. Your brain knows it is doing something effortful.

But here is where it gets important for you specifically. Over time, with repetition, that effort decreases. A study published in the journal Nature Neuroscience tracked what happens in the amygdala — the brain's emotional alarm system — as people lie repeatedly. The first time a person tells a self-serving lie, the amygdala responds strongly. It fires. It signals discomfort, the low-grade unease that most people experience as guilt or anxiety when they are being dishonest. But each subsequent lie about the same thing, or lies of the same type, produces a weaker amygdala response. The signal gets quieter. The discomfort fades. And the brain, which is always looking for ways to be more efficient, begins to treat dishonesty as a default pathway — a well-worn road it knows how to travel without much effort.

The researchers called this process emotional adaptation. You might call it something simpler: you got used to it. And once you got used to it, the lying stopped feeling like a choice and started feeling like just the way things are.

There is also the matter of white matter. A study published in the British Journal of Psychiatry found something striking when it examined the brains of pathological liars — people for whom deception had become a habitual, automatic pattern of behavior. Compared to non-liars, they showed a significant increase in white matter in the prefrontal cortex. White matter is the brain's wiring — the connective tissue that allows different regions to communicate with each other quickly and efficiently. More white matter in a particular pathway means faster, more automatic processing along that pathway. In practical terms: the brains of habitual liars had been physically restructured by the act of lying. They had built infrastructure for it. They had, without ever intending to, trained their brains to deceive the way other people train their bodies to run.

Think about what that means for a moment. You did not start out this way. At some point in your life — as a boy, as a young man, somewhere along the road — you began lying in response to something. Fear, shame, conflict, consequence. And every time you chose the lie over the truth, you were not just making a single bad decision in isolation. You were laying down another strand of wire. Building another connection. Making the next lie slightly faster, slightly more automatic, slightly less costly to your conscience. You were, in the most literal neurological sense, practicing.

You practiced until you were good at it. And now you are wondering why you cannot seem to stop.

This is the habit loop of deception, and it works the same way every other habit works. There is a trigger — something that creates discomfort, threat, or anxiety. There is a behavior — the lie, the omission, the half-truth, the deflection. And there is a reward — the relief of having avoided the confrontation, the momentary safety of having kept the secret intact. That relief is real. It is felt in the body. And the brain, which is engineered to seek relief and avoid pain, files that sequence away: when this situation arises, do that thing, get that result. Over years, over thousands of repetitions, the loop becomes grooved so deeply that the behavior triggers before the conscious mind has had a chance to weigh in.

This is why men who genuinely want to stop lying often find that they have already told another lie before they even realized they were doing it. They come to a coaching session or a therapy appointment and say, with complete sincerity, "I don't even know why I said it. I didn't plan to lie. It just came out." And they are telling the truth about that — the lie did just come out, because the neural pathway for it is faster and more established than the pathway for the honest response. The habit is running the show while the conscious, well-intentioned part of the brain is still catching up.

Understanding this does not let you off the hook. But it does explain why resolve alone is not enough. You cannot simply decide to stop and have that decision hold. You have to actively build new pathways. You have to practice honesty the same way you accidentally practiced deception — repeatedly, in low-stakes situations, until the honest response starts to become the one that comes naturally. That process takes time. It takes discomfort. And it will not work at all if you skip the part where you understand exactly what you are up against.

There is another dimension to this that does not get talked about enough, and it is the one I have found most useful in coaching rooms. It is the relationship between lying and self-deception — which is to say, the lies you tell yourself, not just the ones you tell other people.

The brain is not a neutral recording device. It is a meaning-making machine, and one of the things it is most motivated to do is protect the story you have constructed about who you are. Psychologists call this cognitive dissonance — the discomfort of holding two contradictory beliefs at the same time. For most men who lie habitually, there is a significant gap between their self-image and their behavior. They see themselves as good men, decent men, men who love their families. And they are also doing things that good, decent, family-loving men do not do. That gap is intolerable to the brain. So the brain does what it always does when faced with intolerable discomfort — it closes the gap, not by changing the behavior, but by rewriting the story.

And so the lies become justified. "I work hard, I provide for this family, I deserve this." "She wouldn't understand anyway, so what's the point of telling her." "It's not hurting anyone." "Every man does this." "If she were more attentive, more present, more of what I needed, I wouldn't be in this position." These are not random thoughts. These are the brain performing self-protective maintenance — keeping the story of the good man intact even as the behavior contradicts it at every turn. And the more the brain practices this rewriting, the more convincing it becomes — not just to other people, but to the man himself.

This is the most dangerous form of lying there is. Because the man who has lied to himself long enough genuinely believes his own justifications. He has lost the ability to clearly see what he is doing and why. He is not pretending when he says he does not understand why things fell apart. He has edited the internal record so thoroughly that the truth is genuinely hard for him to access. I have sat with men in this state and watched them be confused by their own behavior — men who cheated for years and then could not explain it, not because they were performing confusion, but because the explanation had been buried under years of self-directed dishonesty.

There is a phrase I use in coaching that I want to give you now, and I want you to hold onto it as you move through this book. The phrase is this: the first lie is always the one you tell yourself.

Every pattern of deception in a marriage has a corresponding pattern of self-deception that predates it. You lied to her about where you were because you had already lied to yourself about what you were doing and why. You lied to her about the money because you had already lied to yourself about whether you had a problem. You lied to her about how you felt about the marriage because you had already lied to yourself about how far gone things actually were. The external lie is almost always downstream of an internal one. Fix the internal one, and the external lies start to lose their foothold.

This is not easy to hear, because it means that the work of becoming an honest man is not just about learning to say true things out loud. It is about learning to see true things clearly, inside your own head, before they ever reach your mouth. It is about developing the willingness to sit with a reality you do not like rather than immediately reaching for a more comfortable reframe. It is about tolerating the discomfort of cognitive dissonance — holding both things at once, "I am a man who wants to be good" and "I am a man who has done harm" — without immediately collapsing one of them to escape the tension.

That tolerance is a skill. It can be built. But it requires that you first accept that the brain you are working with is not a neutral ally in this process. It has been shaped by years of practice in a direction you now want to reverse. It will resist. It will offer you justifications. It will make the familiar feel safe and the honest feel dangerous. Knowing that this is happening — understanding the mechanism — is the first step toward not being run by it.

I want to tell you about a man named Derek, because Derek illustrates something important about where this goes when it is left unchecked. Derek was forty-three when I first worked with him, and he had been managing a double life for six years. He was a meticulous man — detail-oriented, careful, someone who prided himself on his discipline and competence. He had separate email accounts, a second phone that he kept in his car, an elaborate system of cover stories that had evolved over the years to handle every possible contingency. He had, in other words, put enormous intelligence and energy into maintaining his deception.

What Derek said to me in our first session has stayed with me for years. He said: "I'm actually a very honest person. I hate liars. I've always hated liars. I don't know how I ended up here."

He was not performing when he said that. He was not trying to manipulate me. He genuinely believed it. The brain's capacity for self-deception had been so thorough, so efficient, that Derek had managed to sustain a six-year architecture of lies while still maintaining a self-image as an honest man. The two things existed in separate compartments, and the brain had been careful never to let them meet.

The work we did together was not primarily about stopping the affair. The affair stopped almost as a byproduct of the real work, which was dismantling the compartmentalization — forcing Derek to hold his behavior and his self-image in the same room at the same time, without allowing the brain to separate them again. It was one of the most difficult things I have ever watched a man do. It was also one of the most important.

Because until Derek could see himself clearly — not the version he wanted to believe in, not the version that felt most defensible, but the actual version, the one that had been making real decisions with real consequences — he could not change. Self-deception is not a refuge. It is a prison. And the bars are invisible, which makes them harder to find and harder to break.

Let me bring this chapter down to the most practical place I can, because all of this neuroscience means nothing if you cannot use it.

What you need to understand is that your lying is not simply a moral failing. It is a deeply ingrained neurological pattern that was built over time and has been reinforced with every repetition. It lives in your body as much as in your mind. It has altered the physical structure of your brain in ways that make honesty feel more difficult and deception feel more natural than it should. You did not choose this consciously. But you did build it. And because you built it, you can rebuild it in a different direction. That process is possible. I have watched it happen, in men who were far more entrenched than you may be right now.

But the rebuilding requires something that does not come naturally to men who have spent years in self-protection mode. It requires honesty about the dishonesty. It requires the willingness to look at the pattern clearly — not to feel devastated by it, not to perform remorse, but to see it accurately, the way a doctor looks at an X-ray. This is what is broken. This is how it got broken. This is what it will take to fix it.

Your brain rewired itself to lie. You are going to spend the rest of this book learning how to rewire it back. Not to the man you were before all of this started — you cannot go back, and you would not want to, because the man you were before was already heading here. To the man you are capable of being. The one who does not flinch from the truth. The one who does not need to manage, calculate, and perform his way through a marriage. The one who can sit across from his wife and say what is real without his heart hammering in his chest.

That man exists. He is in there under all the wiring. We are going to find him.

CHAPTER 3

THE WEB YOU WOVE: HOW ONE LIE BECOMES A THOUSAND

It starts with one. That is the part men always forget when they are standing in the wreckage of a marriage, trying to explain how things got so far. They forget that there was a beginning. A single moment, a single decision, a single sentence that was not true. It felt small at the time. It probably was small at the time. A minor misdirection. A detail adjusted. A question answered with just enough truth to pass.

Nobody got hurt. Nothing fell apart. In fact, the remarkable thing about that first lie is how completely unremarkable it seemed. Life went on. The conversation moved forward. And the man who told it filed it away and thought, if he thought about it at all, that it was a one-time thing. A necessary exception to a rule he still believed he lived by.

What he did not understand — what almost no man understands in that moment — is that he had just laid the first strand of a web. And that webs, by their nature, do not stay small.

I worked with a man named Thomas for nearly two years. He was thirty-eight when we started, an engineer by training, which meant he was someone who understood systems, who thought in terms of cause and effect, who prided himself on being logical and precise. He had a wife he described as his best friend, two daughters he coached at soccer, and a relationship with a woman from his gym that had started, in his telling, almost by accident.

When Thomas first came to see me, he had been managing the affair for three years. And he had been doing it, in his words, cleanly. No major slipups. No close calls he had not been able to smooth over. He had a system. He had thought through most of the contingencies. And he was exhausted in a way that had nothing to do with how much he was sleeping.

In our early sessions, I asked Thomas to do something that made him uncomfortable. I asked him to trace it all the way back to the first lie. Not the affair — the lie. The very first untrue thing he had said to his wife in relation to any of this. He thought about it for a long time. Then he said: "I told her I was staying late for a project review. It was a Thursday. I was actually having dinner with her. Just dinner. Nothing had happened yet."

That was it. A Thursday evening. A project review that did not exist. At that point the relationship was still just a friendship that he sensed was becoming something more, and he did not want to have the conversation with his wife about why he was having dinner with this particular woman. So he simplified it. He erased it. He replaced it with something that would not require explanation.

One lie. Told to avoid one uncomfortable conversation. That was the first strand.

By the time Thomas sat across from me three years later, that single strand had become something he could no longer count. Hundreds of individual deceptions, large and small. A second phone. A locked email account. A running mental inventory of what he had told his wife versus what he had told his colleagues versus what he had told his mother on the phone about why he sometimes seemed distracted.

He had built a management system for his lies — not because he was a criminal mastermind, but because the web had grown complex enough that managing it had become a part-time job. And like all systems under increasing load, it was beginning to crack.

This is the architecture of deception, and it follows a logic so consistent that I have seen it replicate almost identically across hundreds of different men in hundreds of different circumstances. The first lie creates a gap between what is real and what the other person believes. That gap must be maintained. Maintaining it requires a second lie — not necessarily a big one, just something to keep the gap from closing.

The second lie creates a slightly larger and more complex gap, which requires more maintenance. And so on, and so on, compounding with every iteration, until the man at the center of it is spending more mental energy on the management of his deception than he is on anything else in his life.

Psychologists who study deception describe this as the cognitive load of lying — the mental tax that deception places on the person doing it. Holding a false reality in your head while simultaneously navigating the true one is genuinely demanding work. You have to remember not just what you said, but who you said it to, when you said it, what level of detail you used, and what follow-up questions might naturally arise from it.

You have to track the consistency of your stories across conversations that may be separated by days or weeks. You have to stay alert to anything that might cause the two realities to collide — a comment your wife makes that suggests she knows something, a text that comes through on the wrong phone, a date that does not line up with something you said six months ago.

This is not a sustainable way to live. And the body knows it, even when the conscious mind is still telling itself it has everything under control. The chronic low-grade stress of maintaining a web of lies registers in the nervous system the same way any sustained threat does.

Elevated cortisol. Disrupted sleep. A baseline of hypervigilance that makes it difficult to ever fully relax, even in moments that should be safe. Men in the middle of long-running deceptions frequently describe a feeling they cannot quite name — a tightness, a restlessness, a sense that something is always slightly wrong even when nothing specific is happening. That feeling is the body sending a message the mind has been refusing to receive. It is the cost of the web, paid in increments, every single day.

There is something else that happens inside a marriage when the web grows large enough, and it is the thing that breaks trust in a way that is very difficult to repair. It is what researchers in couples therapy call the contamination effect.

When a person is deceived by someone they love and trusted, and the deception is eventually uncovered, they do not simply lose trust in the specific things they were lied to about. They lose trust in the entire history of the relationship. Every memory becomes suspect. Every good moment gets held up to the light and examined for hidden meaning.

She thinks: Was he lying then, too? Was any of it real? Did he mean what he said on our wedding day, or was that performance as well? The discovery of a lie does not just damage the present. It reaches backward through time and poisons the past.

This is what men almost never anticipate when they are in the middle of managing their deceptions. They think about discovery in terms of the current situation — the specific thing they are hiding, the specific conversation they are dreading. They do not think about the way their wife will go back through fifteen years of marriage with a different set of eyes once she knows.

They do not think about the fact that every moment she believed she understood — every vacation, every difficult season they got through together, every time he said I love you and she believed him — will become a question she cannot answer with any confidence. The web does not just trap the present. It retroactively traps everything that came before it.

I have watched women sit in that realization in real time, during sessions where the truth was finally being told. It is one of the most painful things I have ever witnessed. Not the anger — the anger comes later and it is in many ways easier to be in the room with. It is the confusion. The disorientation of a person whose entire framework for understanding her own life has just been taken from her. She is not just grieving the betrayal. She is grieving every version of reality she believed in that now turns out to have been, at least in part, constructed.

If you have children, understand this: they absorb this disorientation too. They may not know the details. But children are extraordinarily sensitive to the emotional weather of a home, and a home where one parent is carrying a sustained deception and the other is beginning to sense that something is wrong is a home with a particular kind of tension that children feel in their bodies even when they cannot name it. The web does not just affect your marriage. It affects everything that lives inside it.

Let me talk about something that does not get enough attention in conversations about lying, which is the particular damage done by lies of omission. These are the quieter entries in the web — the things not said, the details left out, the questions answered with a technically accurate statement that leaves a false impression. Men are often especially skilled at this form of deception, and they use it to maintain a kind of internal defense: I did not lie. I just did not tell her everything.

That defense does not hold. Omission is lying. Not legally, not in some abstract philosophical sense, but in the specific practical sense that matters in a marriage — which is this: a lie is anything you do or say with the intention of causing your partner to believe something that is not true. It does not matter whether you constructed the false impression with an active statement or a deliberate silence. The intention and the effect are the same. She believed something that was not accurate, because you chose to let her believe it. That is deception, full stop.

Men who rely heavily on omission often tell themselves they are being kind — that they are sparing their wife from painful information she does not need. And occasionally that is partially true.

There are things in a marriage that do not need to be said, details that belong to a private interior life and do not rise to the level of requiring disclosure. But that is not what I am talking about, and you know it is not what I am talking about.

The omissions that matter, the ones that belong in this conversation, are the ones where the withheld information would change how your wife understands her own life. Those omissions are not kindness. They are control. They are the decision, made unilaterally, that she does not get to know the truth about the reality she is living in. And that decision belongs in the web right alongside everything else.

Thomas, the engineer, eventually told his wife everything. Not in one conversation — it took several, spread over a difficult month, each one more complete and more costly than the one before. He described the experience as simultaneously the most terrifying and the most relieving thing he had ever done. The terrifying part was obvious. The relieving part surprised him.

He said: "I kept waiting for the other shoe to drop. For three years, I kept waiting. And the horrible thing is, I didn't even realize I was waiting until

I finally stopped. Until there was nothing left to hide. And then I felt it — this thing lifting. This weight I'd been carrying so long I'd stopped noticing it was there."

His marriage did not survive intact. They separated for a period. They went through couples therapy. Whether they ultimately rebuild what they had is still being determined as of the time I am writing this. But Thomas himself — as a man, as a person — is more present than he has been in years. More available to his daughters. More honest in every conversation, not just the ones with his wife. The web held him as much as it held anything else. When it came down, he came with it, back to something that felt more like solid ground.

Here is what I want you to carry out of this chapter.

The lie you are telling yourself right now — the one you have decided is manageable, necessary, contained — is not any of those things. It is a living thing. It grows. It requires feeding. It connects to other lies and builds structures you did not plan and cannot fully see. Every day you maintain it, you are adding another strand to the web, making it more complex, making it harder to dismantle, making the eventual reckoning — and there will be one, because there always is — more costly and more complete.

There is no such thing as a sustainable lie in a marriage. There is only a lie that has not yet finished growing. The man who thinks he has it under control is the man who has not yet seen how big it has gotten, because he is standing in the middle of it.

Step back. Look at it honestly. Count the strands, if you can bear to count them. Not to destroy yourself with what you find. But to understand, with the full weight of clarity, exactly what you have built and exactly what it is going to take to undo it.

Because you can undo it. Not erase it — the web leaves marks, and pretending otherwise would be its own kind of lie. But you can stop building. You can start clearing. You can choose, starting now, not to add a single new strand.

That choice, made and held, is where everything else begins.

PART 2

WHY YOU REALLY LIE

CHAPTER 4

THE MAN BEHIND THE MASK: IDENTITY AND SELF-DECEPTION

There is a question I ask every man I work with, usually in the second or third session, once the surface-level story has been told and we are ready to go somewhere more honest. I ask it plainly, without setup, because I have found that the way a man responds to it in the first few seconds — before he has had a chance to compose an answer — tells me more than almost anything else he will say.

The question is this: Who are you when no one is watching?

Most men pause. Some of them laugh, a little uncomfortably. Some of them look at the floor. A few of them — the ones who have been carrying their deception the longest — get a look in their eyes that is somewhere between recognition and grief, as if the question has reached through the performance and touched something they had almost forgotten was there. And then they start to answer. And almost always, the answer is more complicated than they expected it to be. Because the man who has been lying for years has often lost clear sight of the line between who he actually is and who he has been pretending to be. The two have blurred. The mask has been on so long it has started to feel like a face.

We all wear masks. That is not a confession of wrongdoing — it is a description of how human beings navigate social life. You are a slightly different version of yourself at work than you are at home. You present differently to your parents than you do to your friends. You have a public self and a private self, and the gap between them is not inherently dishonest. Some of that gap is simply context, the natural adjustment of presentation that every socially functional person makes.

But there is a different kind of mask. The one that is not about context but about concealment. The one that is worn not because different situations call for different versions of you, but because the true version of you — the one with the desires you are ashamed of, the failures you have not admitted, the doubts and fears and hungers you have never spoken aloud — feels too dangerous to show anyone. Including yourself.

This is the mask I am talking about. And the man who wears it long enough stops being able to feel the weight of it. He stops noticing the effort it takes to maintain it. He stops asking himself what is underneath it, because the question has become too threatening. He builds his entire identity around the surface — the good husband, the reliable provider, the man who has it together — and defends that identity with the ferocity of someone who knows, somewhere beneath conscious awareness, that it is not entirely real.

Friedrich Nietzsche, who was one of the more unflinching observers of human nature who ever put pen to paper, wrote that the most common lie is the one a man tells himself. Not the lies we construct for other people — those are almost always downstream of something deeper. The primary act of deception in a dishonest life is internal. It is the story we tell ourselves about who we are, why we do what we do, and what it means. Every external lie has a corresponding internal one that made it possible. You cannot consistently deceive someone else about your life without first deceiving yourself about it.

This is what psychologists mean when they talk about self-deception, and it is more sophisticated and more dangerous than it sounds. Self-deception is not simply ignorance. It is not that you do not know what is true. At some level, usually a level just below comfortable awareness, you do know. You know what you are doing. You know what it means. You know what it is costing. But the knowledge is intolerable, so the mind buries it — not deeply enough to fully disappear, but deeply enough to be livable.

You carry it the way you carry a low-grade fever. You are aware of it without ever quite confronting it. And so you function. You go to work and come home and sit at the dinner table and say grace and help with homework and make love to your wife and all the while there is this thing underneath everything, this knowledge you have agreed with yourself not to look at directly.

That agreement — the silent deal you made with yourself to not see what you see — is the foundation of everything we are trying to dismantle in this book. Because you cannot change what you will not acknowledge. And you cannot acknowledge what you have carefully constructed a life around not seeing.

I want to talk about identity, because identity is what is really at stake in all of this. Not your marriage, not your reputation, not even your relationship with your children — though all of those matter enormously and we will get to them. Identity is the deeper thing. It is the answer to the question of who you are. And for a man who has been lying, that question has become genuinely difficult to answer.

Here is how the identity problem develops. A man starts with a self-concept — a story about who he is. He is a good man. A faithful man. A man of integrity. These are not just labels he has applied to himself. They are things he believes, at a foundational level, about his own character.

They are load-bearing. They hold up the structure of how he moves through the world and how he sleeps at night.

Then he does something that contradicts the story. He lies. He cheats. He hides. He does something the good faithful man of integrity would not do. And now there is a problem — not just a practical problem, but an existential one. He cannot simultaneously be the man he believes himself to be and the man he is currently behaving as. The two cannot coexist without causing a kind of internal earthquake.

So the mind does what it always does when faced with unbearable contradiction. It resolves it. Not by changing the behavior — that would require too much. By adjusting the story. By finding a way to make the behavior fit within the framework of the good man identity. By building a set of justifications and rationalizations that serve as the mortar between the cracks. He tells himself: this is an exception. This is temporary.

This is complicated in ways other people would not understand. She drove me to this. The marriage was already broken. I give so much in every other area of my life that I deserve this one thing. I am still a good man, just a good man in a hard situation.

These are not random thoughts. They are identity protection. They are the mind fighting to preserve the self-concept against the evidence of the behavior. And they are remarkably effective — not at solving anything, but at allowing a man to continue doing what he is doing without having to fully reckon with what it means about who he is. The justifications are the internal lies that make the external ones possible. They are the scaffolding that holds the mask in place.

I worked with a man named Raymond who had been having an affair for eighteen months when his wife found a receipt in his jacket pocket. He was a deacon in his church. He coached youth basketball. He was, by every external measure, a pillar of his community — exactly the kind of man who makes you believe that the people who seem most trustworthy are trustworthy. When the truth came out, the people in his life were stunned. Not just hurt. Stunned. Because the Raymond they knew and the Raymond who had been living this double life seemed to be two completely different people.

In my sessions with Raymond, what we had to excavate was not the affair itself but the identity structure that had allowed it to coexist with the rest of his life. Raymond had managed the contradiction by keeping the two worlds hermetically sealed from each other in his mind.

The man who sat in the front pew and the man who drove across town on Tuesday evenings were, in his internal architecture, different people. He had compartmentalized so completely that he could move between those two identities with almost no friction, because he had made sure they never had to meet.

This is what psychologists call compartmentalization, and it is one of the most powerful and destructive tools the human mind has for managing the gap between who we are and who we believe ourselves to be. It allows a man to be genuinely loving with his children in the morning and genuinely dishonest with his wife by afternoon without experiencing the full weight of the contradiction. Each compartment is real. Each one contains real feelings, real experiences, real investments. But they are kept separate by an internal partition that the man maintains, usually without consciously deciding to, as a matter of psychological survival.

The problem with compartmentalization is that the partitions are not permanent. They degrade over time. The friction between the two identities — the one that is performing goodness and the one that is actively causing harm — builds slowly, like pressure behind a dam. Men in long-running deceptions begin to feel it as a diffuse restlessness, an irritability they cannot source, a numbness that settles over the parts of their life that used to feel alive. The compartments are holding, but the holding is costing them everything they are not busy spending on the lie.

Here is the most important thing I can tell you about identity and self-deception, and I want you to read it slowly because it is easy to hear and easy to miss at the same time. The mask is not who you are. But the man who put it on is.

What I mean by that is this: you are not defined by the lies you have told. You are not reducible to the worst version of your behavior. The man who lies is not simply a liar, any more than the man who makes a selfish decision is simply a selfish person. Human beings are more complicated than their worst moments, and one of the things I have learned from sitting with so many men in crisis is that the capacity for genuine change is almost always present, even when it seems most buried.

But the man who made the choices that led here — who built the mask, who chose the deception over and over again, who maintained the compartments and told himself the justifications — that man is also you. Not a separate self. Not a version of you that appeared from nowhere and started making decisions without your consent. You. Your fears, your hungers, your needs, your wounds, your choices. All of it belongs to you. And until you can stand in front of the mirror and see both things at once — the man you want to be and the man who has been doing this — you are not ready to change. Because change requires owning the thing you are changing from.

This is where a lot of men get stuck. They are willing to feel remorse for what they have done. Remorse is, in some ways, the easier part — it is painful, but it is passive. It is feeling bad about something. What is harder, and what actually matters, is ownership. Ownership is saying: I did this. Not my circumstances. Not my wife's failures. Not the pressure of my job or the way I was raised or the particular vulnerability of that moment. I did this. I made these choices. And I am going to make different ones.

That kind of ownership is not self-destruction. It is not about collapsing under the weight of guilt. It is about standing up straight under the weight of truth and deciding that you are the kind of man who can carry it. That is not weakness. That is the most honest form of strength there is.

There is a concept in personal development work called the integrated self — the idea of a person who does not need to manage different identities for different audiences because there is only one identity, consistent across contexts, honest about its nature, clear about its values and its failures both. Integration does not mean perfection. An integrated man still makes mistakes.

He still has parts of himself he is working on. But he is not divided. He is not performing. He is not managing a gap between who he shows the world and who he actually is. He is simply himself, in all his imperfect reality, without apology and without concealment.

That is what we are working toward. Not the man who never struggled. Not the man who pretended he did not have the hungers and the fears and the moments of weakness that every man has. The man who knows himself clearly enough to be honest about all of it. The man whose inside life and outside life are finally, after years of managed distance, the same life.

That man is quieter than the masked man. He does not need to perform. He does not need to manage impressions or track stories or calculate what to reveal. He is, in the deepest sense, free. Not free from consequences — the consequences of what has already happened will take time to work through and some of them will be permanent. But free from the exhausting, soul-draining labor of being two men at once.

Before we move on, I want to ask you to do something honest and uncomfortable. I want you to think about the mask you wear — not in vague terms, but specifically. What is it made of? What does it show the world? What does it hide? If your wife could see clearly the gap between who you present yourself to be and who you actually are in the private spaces of your behavior and your mind, what would she find there? Not to punish you with the answer. But to know it yourself, as clearly as possible, before we go any further.

Because here is what I have found, in room after room with man after man: the gap is almost never as unforgivable as the man believes it to be. What lives in the hidden places is usually not monstrousness. It is fear, and hunger, and woundedness, and failure — human things, things that could be spoken and worked with if a man had the courage to bring them into the light. The mask was built to protect something that did not need protecting the way he thought it did. It was built by a frightened version of him who did not yet know that honesty was survivable.

It is survivable. More than survivable. On the other side of it is the only version of your life that is actually yours. Take the mask off. Not all at once — we will get to the how of that. But start by admitting it is there. Start by looking at it clearly. Start by understanding that the man behind it is the one this book is written to. Not the performance. Not the version built for other people's consumption. The real one. The scared one. The one who still, underneath everything, wants to be someone worth knowing.

That man is who we are working with. And that man, it turns out, is more than enough to build something real from.

CHAPTER 5

WHAT YOU'RE REALLY PROTECTING

When I ask a man why he lied, he almost never says the true thing first. What he says first is one of a handful of answers that have become so common in my work that I could write them on a card and hold them up before the words are even out of his mouth. He says he did not want to hurt her. He says things were complicated and she would not have understood. He says the marriage was already struggling and the truth would have made things worse. He says he was trying to protect the family. He says he panicked. He says he just could not find the right moment to be honest, and the longer it went on, the harder it became.

These answers are not lies, exactly. They contain real feelings. The desire not to hurt someone you love is real. The fear of an impossible conversation is real. The sense that timing matters and the right moment keeps not arriving — that is real too. I am not dismissing any of it.

But none of it is the whole truth. And if you sit with a man long enough, if you push past the first layer of explanation and then the second and then the third, what you eventually find underneath all of it is something much simpler and much harder to say out loud. What you find is this: he was protecting himself. Not her. Not the family. Not the marriage. Himself. His comfort, his access, his image, his options. The lie was in his service, first and last, regardless of how it was packaged when he told it.

This chapter is about that. About seeing clearly, without the softening filter of good intentions, what you were actually protecting when you chose deception over truth. Because until you can name it accurately, you cannot address it. And until you address it, the lying will find new forms even after you think you have stopped.

Let me give you the list. Not to humiliate you, but because naming things precisely is the only way to deal with them. When men lie in their marriages, they are almost always protecting one or more of the following things.

They are protecting their comfort. The truth is uncomfortable. It creates tension, conflict, difficult conversations, and emotional labor. Lying, in the short term, eliminates all of that. The man who lies to avoid a hard conversation is not protecting his wife from pain. He is protecting himself from the discomfort of being the cause of her pain. Those are not the same thing. One is consideration. The other is cowardice dressed in consideration's clothing.

They are protecting their access. Access to the affair, to the behavior, to whatever it is they are hiding. As long as the lie holds, the thing the lie is covering can continue. The man who tells himself he is lying to protect his wife is often, at a more accurate level of analysis, lying to protect his ability to keep doing what he is doing. The lie is not a shield for her. It is a gate that he controls, keeping her out of a part of his life he is not ready to give up.

They are protecting their image. This one runs deep, especially for men who have constructed an identity around being seen a certain way — dependable, good, strong, admirable. The truth, if it came out, would damage that image. People would see something in him that contradicts the version he has spent years building. And because so much of his sense of self is tied to how others perceive him, the threat to the image feels like a threat to the self. So he lies. Not to protect her from knowing. To protect himself from being known.

They are protecting their options. Some men lie not because they have fully committed to a course of action but because they have not yet decided what they want to do. The lie buys time. It keeps the marriage intact while they figure out whether they are going to stay or go. It keeps the affair available while they assess whether it is worth the cost. It maintains the status quo while the man postpones the reckoning that honesty would force. This is perhaps the most cynical form of deception, because the person being lied to is being used — her trust is being leveraged to extend a period of indecision that she does not even know she is funding.

They are protecting their peace. And by peace I mean the absence of consequences. The man who lies to avoid conflict is not a peacemaker. He is a conflict avoider, which is a very different thing. A peacemaker builds genuine resolution. A conflict avoider simply defers the explosion, at the cost of everything that honesty might have repaired. The marriage does not become more peaceful because he withheld the difficult truth. It becomes more brittle. The unspoken thing does not disappear. It accumulates.

I want to spend a moment on the most seductive lie that men tell themselves about their deception, because it is the one I encounter most often and the one that does the most damage precisely because it sounds so noble. The lie is: I am doing this to protect her.

I have heard this from men who were hiding affairs, men who were hiding financial disasters, men who were hiding addictions, men who were hiding the simple fact that they were deeply unhappy in their marriages and did not know how to say so. In almost every case, the protection narrative was sincerely believed, at least on the surface. These were not men cynically hiding behind altruism. They genuinely felt, at some level, that the truth would be worse for her than the lie.

But let me ask you something directly, and I want you to answer it honestly. If the lie truly were about protecting her — if her wellbeing were genuinely the primary consideration — then why does the lie also happen to be the option that is most convenient for you? Why does the protective choice always line up so neatly with the choice that avoids the most consequences for the man making it? That alignment is not a coincidence. It is a tell. When the thing that protects her is also, every single time, the thing that protects you, you are not making a selfless calculation. You are making a selfish one and calling it something else.

Real protection — genuine care for another person's wellbeing — sometimes requires you to say the hard thing even when saying it costs you enormously. A doctor who withholds a diagnosis to spare a patient distress is not being kind. He is being negligent. The kindness is in the truth, delivered with as much care and skill as possible, because the truth is what allows the person to make real decisions about their real life. Your wife deserves to make real decisions about her real life. When you lie to protect her, you are not protecting her. You are managing her. You are deciding, without her consent, what reality she is allowed to live in. That is not love. That is control.

There is a man I worked with named Jerome who had hidden a gambling problem from his wife for four years. Not a recreational hobby — a full clinical addiction that had cost them, by the time I met him, nearly sixty thousand dollars in savings, a second mortgage on the house he had taken out without her knowledge, and three separate loan arrangements with people she had never heard of. Jerome had constructed an elaborate financial fiction to conceal all of it. Fake investment statements. A side business that existed only on paper. A set of explanations for why their savings account balance kept declining that ranged from market volatility to necessary home repairs.

When I asked Jerome why he had not told his wife the truth at any point during those four years, he said what they almost always say. "I didn't want to worry her. She has anxiety. She would have panicked." I sat with that for a moment. Then I asked him: "Did she have any anxiety during those four years?"

He admitted that she had. Significant anxiety, actually. She had been to her doctor about it twice. She had started taking medication for it. She had told Jerome multiple times that she just felt a persistent sense that something was off, that things were not adding up, that there was a tension in their house she could not explain. She had attributed it to work stress, to getting older, to a vague hormonal shift her doctor mentioned. She had blamed herself for feelings that were, in fact, the accurate emotional read of a woman whose nervous system knew she was being deceived even when her conscious mind did not.

Jerome's wife was not being protected from anxiety. She was being given anxiety and then denied the information that would have allowed her to understand it and address it. The lie did not spare her distress. It manufactured distress and then stripped her of any ability to make sense of it or respond to it. She was suffering from a wound she did not know she had, because the man who inflicted it had convinced himself that hiding the knife was an act of love.

This is what the protection narrative actually produces. Not protection. Confusion, anxiety, self-doubt, and a growing sense of unreality in a woman who is being gaslit — not necessarily intentionally, but effectively — by the ongoing maintenance of a false picture of her life.

I also want to address the man who is not protecting an affair or an addiction but something quieter — the man who lies about his emotional life. Who says he is fine when he is not. Who says the marriage is good when it is dying by inches. Who performs contentment and stability because the alternative — admitting that he is lost, or unhappy, or deeply uncertain about things he does not have the language to articulate — feels unbearable.

This man is also lying to protect himself, though the thing he is protecting is different. He is protecting himself from vulnerability. From the terror of being seen in a moment of need. From the cultural programming that told him, from childhood on, that a man who does not have things under control is not much of a man at all. He has learned to perform competence and steadiness so thoroughly that he has lost access to his own interior life. He does not know what he feels most of the time, and what he does feel, he does not trust himself to express without it becoming something he cannot manage.

So he lies by silence. By deflection. By filling the space where honest conversation should be with safe topics, with humor, with the busy-ness of a full life that never quite makes room for depth. And his wife, who is perceptive and who knows him, feels the distance without being able to name it. She tries to close it and he moves, not out of cruelty but out of an old and deeply embedded fear. And the distance grows. And eventually it grows large enough that something fills it that should not have been allowed in. Or it grows large enough that one of them stops trying to close it at all.

This man needs to understand something essential: the vulnerability he is protecting himself from is the same vulnerability that real intimacy requires. You cannot be fully known by someone you will not let see you. And a marriage where two people live in close physical proximity without being fully known to each other is not really a marriage. It is a household.

It is two people managing a shared life without ever quite touching the real life underneath it. That is a loss. Not a catastrophic one, not one that makes headlines, but a profound and daily loss that accumulates over years into something that looks, from the outside, like two people who just grew apart. They did not grow apart. One of them kept moving away.

Here is the question I need you to sit with, and I mean really sit with it — not answer it quickly in your head and move on, but genuinely stay with it for a while.

What are you protecting right now? Not what you tell yourself you are protecting. What are you actually protecting? What is the real thing — the comfort, the access, the image, the option, the peace, the pride — that the lie is in service of? Because there is always a real thing. It is never nothing. And until you can name it clearly and honestly, without the softening of the protection narrative or the justification of complexity, you are not yet at the bottom of this.

The bottom is where the work is. The bottom is where the actual decision lives. Not the decision to stop lying — that is the surface decision, and it matters, but it is not the deepest one. The deepest decision is whether you are willing to stop protecting the thing the lie is protecting. Whether you are willing to give up the comfort, the access, the image, the option, the false peace. Whether you are willing to be inconvenienced, exposed, uncomfortable, and uncertain in the service of becoming someone who lives without the need for the lie.

That is the real cost of honesty. Not the difficult conversation. Not the consequences when the truth comes out. Those are painful but they are temporary. The real cost is giving up the thing you built the lie around. The real cost is becoming a man who no longer has that thing to fall back on. And the real question — the one that determines everything that follows — is whether you are willing to pay it.

CHAPTER 6

WHERE IT STARTED: SECRETS, BOYHOOD, AND WHAT YOU WERE TAUGHT

Nobody is born a liar. That sounds simple, and in some ways it is. But I want you to really hear it, because one of the heaviest things a man carries when he is trying to reckon with a pattern of deception is the belief that this is simply who he is. That the lying is a character trait, something fixed and innate, a permanent feature of his nature rather than a learned behavior with a traceable origin. That belief is not just wrong. It is one of the most effective barriers to change there is, because if the lying is simply who you are, then there is nothing to be done about it. It is like trying to change your height.

But you were not born lying. You learned it. Something in your history — in your family, in your culture, in the specific experiences that shaped the boy you were before you became the man you are — taught you that hiding was safer than being seen, that the managed version of reality was more survivable than the true one. That lesson may have been taught explicitly, through direct instruction or harsh consequence. Or it may have been taught silently, through the atmosphere of the home you grew up in, through what was modeled and what was rewarded and what was punished. However it was delivered, it landed. And you have been living by it ever since.

This chapter is about going back. Not to excuse what you have done — we have been clear about that from the beginning, and we are going to stay clear about it. But to understand it. Because a man who does not understand where his patterns came from is a man who is always at the mercy of them. Understanding the origin does not dissolve the responsibility. It illuminates the path back.

Think about the home you grew up in. Not the holiday-card version of it. The real version. The atmosphere of it — what the air felt like in that house on an ordinary Tuesday evening. What happened when something went wrong. What happened when someone told the truth and the truth was inconvenient or painful or threatening to the image the family maintained for the outside world.

In some homes, truth was met with safety. A child could say I made a mistake or I am scared or I do not know what to do, and what came back was help. Guidance. The experience of being held by someone more capable while you worked through the hard thing. Children who grew up in those homes learned, at a cellular level, that vulnerability was survivable. That honesty led to connection, not punishment. That the people who loved them could handle the real version of who they were.

In other homes — and this is the home I am talking to, because the men who end up in my coaching room did not mostly come from the first kind — truth had consequences. Not always harsh ones. Sometimes the consequence was simply the withdrawal of warmth, the quiet disappointment that landed like a verdict.

Sometimes it was rage. Sometimes it was the suffocating weight of a parent's anxiety, so that telling the truth about something difficult meant absorbing that parent's distress on top of your own. Sometimes it was the unspoken rule that certain things were simply not discussed — that the family had a public face and a private reality, and the gap between them was maintained by a collective, unspoken agreement never to look too directly at the distance.

Boys in those homes learn to edit. They learn to calculate, before speaking, what version of the truth is safe to offer. They learn to read the room with the precision of a diplomat, assessing what their parent can handle today, what the mood in the house will bear, whether this is a moment for honesty or a moment for management. They learn, very early and very efficiently, that the relationship between what they feel and what they say is not a direct one. There is a filter between the interior and the exterior, and maintaining that filter is part of what it means to function in this family.

That filter does not disappear when the boy becomes a man. It moves with him. It sits between him and his wife the same way it sat between him and his parents. It operates by the same logic it always has — protect the relationship by managing what you reveal, keep the peace by keeping the truth at a manageable distance. The habit was built in childhood as a survival strategy. By adulthood it has become so automatic, so deeply embedded in the way a man moves through relationships, that he does not experience it as a choice. He experiences it as just how things are.

I worked with a man named Curtis who grew up in a house where his father's anger was the weather system everything else organized itself around. Not constant rage — that would have been, in its own terrible way, more predictable. His father cycled. There were long stretches of warmth and engagement, of real fathering, followed without warning by periods of cold fury that could be triggered by almost anything and that affected everyone in the house whether they were the direct target or not.

Curtis learned, as children in those environments always do, to become an expert at reading the early signs. A certain set of his jaw. A particular quality of silence over dinner. The way he held his fork.

Curtis became, by necessity, a skilled manager of other people's emotional states. He learned to say what kept the temperature down, to withhold what might spike it, to present himself in whatever configuration was least likely to draw the storm in his direction. He was not being dishonest — he was surviving. The honesty available to him was always conditional, always calculated, always subordinated to the more urgent need to keep things stable.

When Curtis married at twenty-seven, he brought all of that with him. His wife was nothing like his father. She was patient, emotionally generous, genuinely interested in the real version of who he was. But Curtis did not know how to offer her the real version, because he had spent twenty-seven years practicing a different kind of relationship — one built on management rather than openness, on strategic disclosure rather than honest presence. He lied to her not because she gave him reason to but because the lying was all he knew. It was the template. It was home.

His lies were not dramatic at first. Small things. Omissions. The gradual habit of making his interior life unavailable to her, not out of malice but out of an ingrained conviction, learned so young he could not remember learning it, that making yourself fully known to another person was an invitation to pain. Over the years, as the omissions accumulated and the distance they created went unnamed and unaddressed, the lying became larger. Not because Curtis was a bad man. Because an unexamined wound does not stay small.

There is another version of this story, and it is the one that comes from a different kind of household — not the volatile one but the performance one. The family where everything was fine, publicly and permanently.

Where the parents maintained a seamless presentation to the world and asked, implicitly or explicitly, that the children do the same. Where image was the primary currency and anything that threatened the image — failure, struggle, doubt, need — was managed away before it could become visible.

Boys who grow up in performance households learn a particular and sophisticated form of dishonesty. They learn that the outer self and the inner self are two separate projects, and that the outer self is the one that matters. They become adept at presenting well — at being likable, capable, confident, the kind of person others admire. And they become equally adept at concealing everything that does not fit that presentation. Weakness, confusion, failure, need — these things get tucked away, not because anyone explicitly taught them to tuck them away, but because the atmosphere of the home made clear that these things had no comfortable place in the family story.

These men often do not think of themselves as liars. They are just private. They are just professional. They are just the kind of person who does not dump their problems on other people. They have found a hundred socially acceptable ways to describe the habit of emotional concealment, and those descriptions have served them well enough that they have never had to examine what lies underneath them. Until the marriage starts to hollow out from the inside. Until the wife who signed up for a partner finds herself living with a roommate who is excellent at logistics and unavailable for everything else.

Culture has a hand in this too, and I would be doing you a disservice if I did not name it plainly. The culture most men in this country grew up in — regardless of race, regardless of economic background, with some variation but with remarkable consistency across those variables — taught boys that emotional expression is femininity and femininity is weakness. Taught them that a real man handles his own problems without burdening others. Taught them that asking for help is a sign of inadequacy, that uncertainty should be concealed, that pain should be metabolized in private and then performed away in public.

These are not fringe messages. They are woven into the fabric of how boys are raised, how male friendship works, how men are portrayed in virtually every form of entertainment and cultural narrative available to them. The stoic provider. The man who takes the hit and keeps moving. The guy who is always okay, always capable, always in control.

These archetypes are so deeply embedded that most men have internalized them without ever consciously choosing to. They are not performing stoicism. They are stoicism, at least in how they understand themselves. The idea that they might need something — might be struggling, might be lost, might require help to navigate something they cannot manage alone — genuinely does not compute. Not because they are stupid. Because they were never taught a language for it.

And into that language gap, deception moves very naturally. If you cannot say I am struggling, you say I am fine. If you cannot say I am afraid, you say everything is under control. If you cannot say I have made a terrible mistake and I need help understanding why, you build a system to conceal the mistake and you tell yourself that fixing it quietly, alone, is the honorable path. The lie is not always a moral failure in the first instance. Sometimes it is a failure of vocabulary. A man reaching for words he was never given.

The book of Ephesians puts it this way: "Therefore, putting away falsehood, let each one of you speak the truth with his neighbor, for we are members one of another." Members one of another. The language is communal — the idea being that truth is not just a personal virtue but the connective tissue of relationship itself. When we lie, we do not just damage the other person. We sever something. We withdraw from the membership. We make ourselves an island in a relationship that is supposed to be a continent.

What that scripture does not tell you is how to put away falsehood when falsehood is all you were ever equipped with. How to speak truth when truth was never modeled as safe. How to be a member of something when membership — real membership, the kind that requires full presence and honest disclosure — was never demonstrated in the home that first taught you what relationships were.

That is the gap this chapter is trying to close. Not by excusing the lying. But by locating it — by tracing it back to the scared boy who made a very logical decision in a very difficult environment and has been running that decision on autopilot ever since, long after the environment changed and the decision stopped making any sense.

Let me be direct about something that is important to get right. Understanding your history is not the same as being governed by it. Knowing that your father's anger created the template for your conflict avoidance does not mean you are permitted to keep avoiding conflict. Knowing that the performance household you grew up in trained you to separate your interior life from your exterior one does not mean you are allowed to keep operating that separation in your marriage.

Understanding is the beginning of the work, not the end of it. Too many men arrive at the origin story and treat it as a destination — as if understanding why they lie is sufficient reason not to have to change the fact that they do. It is not sufficient. It is a starting point.

It gives you the thread. But following the thread back to where the pattern began is only useful if you then make a different choice going forward. The man who understands his childhood wound and uses it as an explanation for ongoing harmful behavior is not doing healing work.

He is doing excuse work. And if you are honest with yourself, you will know the difference.

The difference is whether the understanding produces change. Whether it makes you more honest, more present, more willing to do the terrifying thing of showing up in your marriage as the full and unedited version of yourself. Whether it creates movement or whether it creates another, slightly more sophisticated layer of justification.

You did not choose the home you grew up in. You did not choose the father you had or the culture you were raised inside or the specific wounds that got inflicted on the boy you were. Those things happened to you. But you are a grown man now. The choices you make from here are yours. The boy who learned to hide in order to survive deserves compassion. The man who keeps hiding when survival no longer requires it deserves a reckoning.

Give the boy the compassion. Give the man the reckoning. Both things can be true at once. In fact, both things have to be true at once, if any of this is going to mean anything.

Go back, if you can, to the earliest memory you have of telling a significant lie. How old were you? What were you afraid of? What did you think would happen if you told the truth? And what actually happened when you did not — when you chose the safer version, the managed version, the version that kept the peace or kept you out of trouble or kept you from having to feel something you did not have the capacity to feel yet?

That memory is where this started. That boy made a decision that made complete sense in the context he was living in. He was doing the best he could with what he had. He deserves to be understood, not condemned. But the decision he made is still running your life. And it is time for the man you have become to review it.

Not everything we learn in childhood is worth keeping. Some of it was survival, not wisdom. Some of it got you through a season it was never meant to last a lifetime. The hiding that protected the boy is destroying the man. And the man — you — is the only one with the power to decide that the lesson is finished and it is time to learn something new.

That is the invitation of this chapter. Not guilt. Not shame. Not another weight to carry. An invitation to understand yourself clearly enough to finally stop being ruled by something you never consciously chose in the first place. You were taught this. You can learn something else.

PART 3

THE COST

CHAPTER 7

WHAT IT'S ACTUALLY COSTING YOU

Men who lie in their marriages tend to think about cost in a very specific and very narrow way. They think about the cost of getting caught. They run calculations about what would happen if the truth came out — the argument, the tears, the possible end of the marriage, the practical upheaval of a life rearranged. They weigh those potential costs against the ongoing cost of maintenance — the vigilance, the tracking, the low-grade stress of keeping things in place — and somewhere in that calculation they have decided, consciously or not, that the current arrangement is still the better deal.

What they almost never do is account for what the lying is already costing them. Right now. Today. Before anyone finds out. Before anything explodes. The costs that are not dramatic, that do not arrive all at once in a single devastating conversation, but that are being paid in small and steady increments every single day that the deception continues.

This chapter is the full accounting. Not the feared future cost. The present, ongoing, already-being-paid cost of living a life built on dishonesty. I want you to look at it clearly, line by line, without the protection of telling yourself it is manageable or temporary or worth it.

Because I have watched too many men reach the end of this road and realize, too late, that they were never as far ahead of the cost as they believed.

The first cost is your integrity, and I mean that in the precise sense of the word — not your reputation, not how others see you, but the internal experience of being a coherent person. Integrity comes from the Latin word for wholeness. A person of integrity is a person whose values, words, and actions are aligned — who is the same person in private that he is in public, who does what he says and says what he means and means what he does. That wholeness is not just a moral achievement. It is a psychological one. It is what allows a man to move through the world without the constant low-grade friction of being at war with himself.

When you lie — when you live in sustained contradiction between who you present yourself to be and what you are actually doing — that wholeness fractures. You become, in a real and felt sense, divided. Not metaphorically divided, but actually divided, the way a bone that has been broken and not set properly develops a false joint. The two halves can move, but they do not move together. There is always friction at the break. And living with that friction, day after day, year after year, extracts a toll from the nervous system that is difficult to measure but impossible to miss if you are honest about what your interior life actually feels like.

Most men in long-running deceptions describe a persistent flatness to their experience — a muting of both pleasure and pain, as if the emotional range has been compressed by the effort of containment. They stop being fully present in the moments that should matter most. They are physically at the dinner table but not actually there. They are in bed with their wife but somewhere else entirely. The lying does not just affect the moments when they are actively deceiving. It seeps into everything. It makes genuine presence almost impossible, because genuine presence requires bringing your full self into the room, and the full self is the one they have been keeping carefully out of sight.

The second cost is your self-respect. This one is harder to admit because admitting it requires acknowledging something most men in active deception are working very hard not to feel. But it is there. Underneath the justifications, underneath the compartmentalization, underneath the carefully maintained story about why this is different and why the usual rules do not quite apply to this particular situation — underneath all of it is a man who, on some level, does not like what he sees when he looks at himself clearly.

Self-respect is not the same as self-esteem. Self-esteem is what you feel about yourself based on how you compare to others, on your accomplishments, on how others respond to you. Self-respect is more basic than that. It is the experience of being someone you can endorse — someone whose choices, when examined honestly, are choices you can stand behind. It does not require perfection. It requires alignment between your values and your actions. And when that alignment is broken, when you are doing things that the deepest part of you knows are wrong, the self-respect drains. Not all at once. Slowly. Quietly. The way a tire goes flat over days rather than in an instant. You might not notice until you are already riding on the rim.

I have watched men in this state try to compensate for the self-respect deficit in ways that do not work. They become hyper-competent at work, achieving more aggressively as if external success can fill the internal gap. They become more generous with money, more present with their children in visible ways — coaching the team, attending every recital — as if public acts of good fathering can offset the private damage of the ongoing deception. They perform goodness harder, because performing goodness harder is easier than being good. And it does not work. The deficit does not close. If anything, the performance makes it worse, because the gap between the performance and the reality becomes one more thing to carry.

The third cost is your marriage — and I mean the living, breathing, daily reality of it, not just the worst-case scenario of it ending. Because the marriage is being damaged right now, today, by the deception, whether or not the deception is ever discovered. Trust, in a marriage, is not just about knowing that your partner is faithful. It is about the accumulative experience of being known — of having offered the real version of yourself and having it received, again and again, over time, until the relationship develops the particular density and warmth that comes from two people who have truly seen each other.

That density cannot develop in the presence of sustained dishonesty. The relationship can look fine from the outside — can have all the right behaviors, the shared meals and the family vacations and the physical intimacy — while remaining fundamentally hollow at its core, because the core requires honest presence and honest presence is exactly what the lying forecloses. Your wife is in a relationship with a version of you. She is building a life with a carefully managed presentation. She is falling asleep next to a man she believes she knows, but the man she knows is not the complete man. And some part of her — the intuitive, body-level knowing that spouses develop over years of close proximity — often senses the gap even when she cannot name it.

This is what produces the low-level disconnection that so many couples in these situations describe without being able to explain. She does not know what is wrong. He does not tell her. She blames herself. He feels guilt that he converts into irritability. She reaches for closeness and encounters something that retreats without explanation. He resents her for asking questions he is afraid to answer honestly. And the marriage slowly hollows out from the inside while the outside remains, to the casual observer, completely intact.

That hollowing is a cost. It is being paid every day. Even if the deception is never discovered, even if the marriage technically survives indefinitely, it survives as a diminished thing — a relationship that had the potential for real depth and intimacy and chose, through the mechanism of sustained dishonesty, to remain permanently on the surface.

The fourth cost is your children. I want to be careful here, because this is the cost that men are most likely to dismiss defensively — to say that the children are fine, that they are protected from all of this, that they do not know and therefore are not affected. That dismissal is wrong, and I am going to tell you why.

Children do not need to know the facts of what is happening to be affected by the emotional reality of it. They are exquisitely sensitive instruments. They read the atmosphere of a home with an accuracy that adults who have learned to rationalize and explain away their perceptions often cannot match.

A child who grows up in a house where one parent is carrying a sustained deception and the other is subconsciously responding to it does not experience that atmosphere as neutral. He experiences it as tension without source, as unease that cannot be located, as the particular anxiety of living in a house where something is wrong but no one will say what it is.

What children learn in that atmosphere is not just an emotional lesson. It is a relational one. They learn what marriage looks like. They learn what honesty looks like in the context of an intimate partnership. They learn whether vulnerability is safe, whether conflict can be navigated openly, whether the people who love each other most are honest with each other. They are building their template for every significant relationship they will ever have, and they are building it from what they observe in you. Not what you tell them. What you do.

A man who lies habitually to his wife is teaching his sons how men behave in marriages. He is teaching his daughters what to expect from the men they will one day choose. He is shaping their attachment patterns, their tolerance for emotional distance, their sense of what love looks and feels like in practice. He is doing all of this without saying a word, simply by being who he is in the house where they are becoming who they will be. That is an enormous responsibility, and it is one that the ongoing deception is actively betraying.

The fifth cost is your health. This one tends to surprise men when I name it, because we do not typically talk about the physical consequences of psychological sustained stress. But the research is clear and it is significant. Chronic stress — the kind produced by maintaining a sustained deception, by the hypervigilance of managing a double life, by the persistent background hum of anxiety that accompanies ongoing dishonesty — has documented physiological effects. Elevated cortisol. Disrupted sleep architecture. Suppressed immune function. Increased inflammatory markers. Elevated blood pressure. These are not metaphors. These are measurable biological consequences of living in sustained psychological conflict.

Men in long-running deceptions frequently report sleep disturbances they attribute to stress without identifying the source of the stress. They report a fatigue that does not respond to rest — a bone-level exhaustion that has less to do with physical exertion than with the relentless cognitive and emotional labor of maintaining the lie. They report a difficulty being fully present even in the moments they most want to be present in, a persistent low-grade distraction that sits between them and their actual experience of their life. These are not character flaws. They are symptoms. They are the body's honest report on what the sustained dishonesty is doing to it.

There is also the drinking, which deserves its own mention because it is so common and so often goes unexamined in this context. Men who are carrying significant deception frequently self-medicate. Not always dramatically — not necessarily in ways that anyone would call a problem. But the glass of whiskey at the end of the day that used to be one is now two or three.

The weekend drinking that used to be social has become something that happens alone, or that starts earlier than it should. The substance is doing the work that the truth should be doing — creating chemical distance from the interior reality that is too uncomfortable to sit with sober. That is a cost too. It compounds everything else.

The sixth cost — and in some ways the most profound one — is the loss of your own life. Not your life in the dramatic sense. In the daily sense. In the sense that your actual experience of being alive — the texture of it, the fullness of it, the access you have to genuine joy and genuine connection and genuine peace — is being consumed by the maintenance of something that is not real.

Think about the mental real estate that the lie occupies. The background processing that never fully stops — the tracking, the calculating, the contingency planning, the monitoring of what you have said and to whom and whether it is still consistent with what else has been said. Think about the conversations you have not been able to be fully present in because part of your mind was somewhere else. The moments with your children you were physically present for but mentally absent from. The times your wife said something real and reached for genuine connection and what she got back was a managed response from a man who could not afford to let her in all the way.

That is your life being spent on something that is not worth it. Those are minutes and hours and days and years of the one existence you are going to get, spent on the labor of maintaining a fiction. And at the end of it — whenever the end comes, whether through discovery or decision or simply the slow death of everything that was once alive in the marriage — you will not get those years back. The man who has lived inside a long deception and finally comes out the other side does not just grieve the damage he has done to others. He grieves the life he did not live while he was busy managing the one he was pretending to have.

That grief is real. I have sat with it in too many rooms to minimize it. And it is, in many ways, the most honest argument for stopping now rather than later. Not because the consequences of discovery will be terrible — though they will. Not because you owe it to your wife or your children — though you do. But because every day you continue is a day of your own life that is not yours. It belongs to the lie. And the lie is a very poor custodian of a human life.

I want to leave you with an image that one of the men I worked with offered me, years ago, after he had come through the worst of his reckoning and was starting to understand what had been happening to him during the years of deception. He said it felt like being underwater. Not drowning — he was functional, he was managing, he was by any external measure above water. But underwater. Everything slightly muffled. Colors slightly muted. Movement slightly labored. The surface of normal life visible above him but always at a slight remove, always requiring just a little more effort to reach than it should.

He said that when he finally told the truth — when the deception ended and the reckoning came and passed and he was standing in the aftermath of it, damaged and exposed and more alone than he had ever been — the first thing he noticed was that he could breathe. That the muffling was gone. That the colors were back. That he was above the surface for the first time in years and the air, even in the middle of all the devastation, tasted like something he had forgotten was possible.

That is what the lying is costing you. The air above the surface. The color of your own life. The ability to be present in the moments that matter, to love without performance, to rest without calculation, to be the full and unmanaged version of yourself in the one life you have been given. The cost is not coming. It is not waiting for you at some future point of reckoning. It is being extracted, every single day, in the currency of your own aliveness. It is time to stop paying it.

CHAPTER 8

THE EXPLOSION: WHAT HAPPENS WHEN SHE FINDS OUT

It comes. It always comes. Maybe it has already come for you, and that is why you are holding this book. Maybe you are in the thick of it right now — the house is still vibrating from it, the conversations are still raw, and you are reading these pages at two in the morning because sleep is not available and you do not know what to do with yourself. Maybe the explosion has not happened yet but you can feel it building, the way you can feel a storm in your joints before the sky changes, and some part of you is bracing for it even as another part of you keeps finding reasons to believe it might not come.

It comes. In twenty years of working with men in deception, I have never encountered a case of sustained marital dishonesty that simply resolved quietly, that just dissolved on its own without a moment of reckoning. Sometimes the reckoning is a dramatic discovery — a text message, a receipt, a phone left unlocked in the wrong moment. Sometimes it is a slow accumulation of evidence that eventually becomes undeniable. Sometimes it is the man himself who breaks, who decides that he cannot carry the weight of it for one more day and sits down and begins to tell the truth before he fully knows why. The form varies. The outcome does not. The truth surfaces. It always does.

This chapter is for the man who is living through the explosion or who is about to. It is also for the man who thinks he is nowhere near one, because he needs to understand what he is building toward regardless of whether he can currently see it from where he is standing.

The first thing that happens when the truth comes out is not what most men expect. They have imagined the explosion in terms of her reaction — the anger, the tears, the accusations. And that is real. That comes. But what men are often completely unprepared for is what happens inside themselves in the moment of discovery.

They expect relief, because they have heard that honesty is a weight lifted, and in time that is true. What arrives first is something that feels more like free fall. The architecture they have been living inside — the managed reality, the careful construction of an alternate version of events — collapses all at once, and the man is suddenly standing in the ruins of it with nothing to hold onto.

The lie was a structure. It was terrible and exhausting, but it was a structure. When it goes, there is a disorientation that is almost physical. Men describe feeling suddenly exposed in a way they cannot quite locate, stripped of something they did not realize they were relying on until it was gone.

That disorientation is important to name, because in the immediate aftermath of discovery, men often respond to it in ways that make everything worse. They minimize. They qualify. They offer partial truths designed to test the waters before committing to the full picture. They watch her reaction carefully, calculating how much to reveal based on how much she seems to already know.

They apologize in ways that are more about managing her distress than genuinely reckoning with the harm they have caused. All of this happens at lightning speed, often without conscious decision, driven by the same automatic self-protective instincts that built the deception in the first place.

The discovery moment is, for most men, the single most important opportunity they will ever have to begin rebuilding — and it is the moment most men waste by immediately going back into self-protection mode. I cannot tell you how many men I have worked with whose marriages might have survived if they had met the moment of discovery with full honesty and full accountability, but who instead offered a managed version of the truth and then had to watch as the trickle-disclosure pattern — more truth coming out in pieces over days and weeks and months — destroyed what remained of their wife's capacity to believe anything they said.

Here is something you need to understand about the experience of being deceived, because understanding it may be the difference between doing this right and doing it wrong at the most critical moment.

When a woman discovers that she has been lied to by her husband, she does not just lose trust in the specific thing she has been lied about. She loses the ground under her feet. She has been operating, for however long the deception has been running, on a set of beliefs about her life that turn out to have been partially or entirely false. She believed she knew who she was married to. She believed she had an accurate picture of her own life. She believed that her read on her relationship — the read that told her things were difficult but basically okay, or basically honest, or basically what they appeared to be — was a reliable one.

All of that disappears in the moment of discovery. And what replaces it is not just pain. It is a fundamental uncertainty about her own perception, her own judgment, her own ability to trust what she sees and knows and feels.

This is what trauma researchers call a shattered assumption — the collapse of the core beliefs that allow a person to navigate life with a baseline sense of safety and predictability. The betrayal of infidelity or sustained deception is classified as a traumatic event not because it is physically dangerous but because it does exactly this — it demolishes the assumptive world, the internal map that tells a person how reality works and what they can count on.

She is not overreacting. She is not being dramatic. She is responding appropriately to the experience of having her reality dismantled, which is one of the more psychologically violent things that can happen to a person in the context of an intimate relationship.

When you understand that, the question "why can't she just move past it?" becomes not just insensitive but genuinely unintelligent. You are asking someone whose map has been destroyed to navigate without one. You are asking someone whose trust in her own perception has been shattered to simply decide to perceive things differently. It does not work that way.

The rebuilding of that internal map takes time — often a great deal of time — and it requires consistent, patient, transparent honesty from the person who destroyed it. There are no shortcuts. There is no speech you can give, no gesture you can make, no single act of contrition that substitutes for the long and unglamorous work of being trustworthy, day after day, until trustworthiness is what the evidence actually shows.

I want to talk about the cycle that most couples fall into after discovery, because it is so consistent and so predictable that I can almost describe it before a man tells me what happened in his house. Therapists who work with couples in infidelity recovery have named it the Lying-Exposure-Explosion cycle, and it works like this: the deception is discovered or disclosed, which produces an explosion — not necessarily a single dramatic confrontation, but a period of acute crisis and emotional upheaval.

The man, overwhelmed by her reaction and his own guilt and the collapse of the structure he had been living inside, manages the explosion rather than addresses it. He offers enough truth to reduce the immediate temperature. He makes promises. He performs remorse. And she, because she loves him and because the alternative is too devastating to fully contemplate, begins to extend something that looks like forgiveness.

But it is not forgiveness. Not yet. It is hope — the hope that what she has been told is the whole story, that the man who is sitting across from her with his head in his hands is the real man and not another performance. And then something comes out. Another detail. Another inconsistency. A piece of information that should have been disclosed in the first conversation but wasn't, that surfaces weeks or months later through a question she thought to ask or something she happened to find. And the explosion happens again. Bigger this time, because now she is not just grieving the original betrayal. She is grieving the betrayal of the disclosure — the discovery that even in his moment of supposed honesty, he was still managing her.

This cycle can repeat four or five or six times in a marriage where the disclosure has been handled through trickle honesty rather than full transparency. And each repetition causes damage that is qualitatively different from and in some ways worse than the original discovery, because each one confirms what she is most afraid to believe: that she still cannot trust what he tells her. That the honesty she was promised was another managed version. That the full truth is something she may never be given.

I have watched marriages survive one explosion, or even two. I have watched very few survive five or six. The trickle is not kindness. It is not strategy. It is the same self-protective instinct that built the deception, still running the show, still choosing the path of least immediate pain over the path of genuine healing. And it destroys the possibility of recovery more reliably than almost anything else.

There is a man I worked with named Victor who discovered, in the most excruciating way possible, what trickle disclosure costs. Victor had been discovered after a two-year affair. In the initial confrontation with his wife, he admitted to the affair but minimized its duration, its depth, and the extent to which he had involved mutual friends in covering for him. He told himself he was protecting her from details that would only cause additional pain without serving any purpose. He told himself that the core truth was what mattered and the periphery was not her business.

Over the following six months, she found out everything. Not because Victor chose to tell her, but because the truth has its own gravity — it surfaces through inconsistencies, through questions that do not get satisfying answers, through the thing a mutual friend lets slip without realizing the full picture has not been shared. Each discovery was a new explosion. Each one reset the clock on whatever fragile progress they had made. By the time Victor finally understood what he had done — not just the affair, but the managed disclosure that followed it — his wife had concluded that she was not capable of trusting anything he said. Not because she did not want to. Because the evidence of his behavior had made trust irrational.

Victor told me: "I thought I was protecting her. I was actually just protecting myself one more time. I told myself it was about her pain, but I wasn't ready to face what full honesty would cost me. So I gave her pieces. And every piece she had to find herself was another proof that I couldn't be trusted. I was still lying while I was trying to stop lying. And I didn't even know it."

That is what the self-protective instinct does when it is left unexamined. It follows you into the reckoning and keeps working, even when every conscious part of you believes you are finally being honest. Let me address something directly that men in the aftermath of discovery often refuse to let themselves hear: her reaction is not the problem.

I say this because the conversation in a coaching room, in the days and weeks after discovery, very often shifts — sometimes subtly, sometimes not — toward her response. She is not handling this well. She is saying things that are unfair. She is punishing him beyond what the situation warrants. She has become someone he does not recognize. He is trying to do the right thing now and she will not let him. He wants to move forward and she keeps pulling everything back to the beginning.

All of this may be true, in the narrow factual sense. She may be saying things that are unfair. She may be responding in ways that are difficult to be on the receiving end of. Grief and betrayal produce responses that are not always measured or proportionate or easy to live with. But the man who has arrived at the conclusion that her reaction is the primary problem he is dealing with has made a significant error in his moral accounting. He has shifted the frame from what he did to how she is responding to what he did. And that shift, however natural it feels, is a continuation of the same self-protective pattern that created the crisis in the first place.

Her reaction belongs to her. It is hers to have. It is the appropriate and human response of a person whose trust has been violated and whose reality has been dismantled. Your job, in this period, is not to manage her reaction or assess its proportionality or determine when it has gone on long enough. Your job is to be the kind of man — consistent, transparent, accountable, patient — whose behavior over time gives her something solid to rebuild on. That is it. That is the whole job. Everything else is distraction.

I also want to speak to the man who has not yet been discovered, who is reading this chapter as a kind of preview of what is coming if he does not change course. I want to say something to him that I mean without any softening.

You are not going to manage your way to safety. The feeling that you have things under control, that you have been careful enough, that the particular shape of your deception is somehow less detectable than most — that feeling is not evidence. It is the same self-deception we talked about in chapter two, now serving its most dangerous function: convincing you that the reckoning is optional when it is only delayed.

The choice available to you right now — and it is a genuine choice, one of the last unilateral ones you will have in this situation — is whether the truth comes out on your terms or on someone else's. Whether you are the one who chooses to tell it, with whatever degree of care and context and genuine contrition you can bring to it, or whether it surfaces through a text message and a locked phone and a Friday evening that starts with dinner and ends with everything falling apart in a way you did not get to prepare for and cannot control.

Discovery without disclosure is the worst version of this. It takes the hardest conversation there is and strips you of any agency in how it happens. It positions you, from the very first moment, as the man who did not choose honesty — the man who had to have it forced from him. That is a position it is very difficult to recover from, not because she will necessarily make that choice impossible, but because you will have confirmed, in the starkest possible way, the thing she will already be wondering: whether you are someone who tells the truth when it matters, or only when you have no other option.

There is a harder and braver path. It is the path of choosing disclosure before discovery. Of being the one who comes to her, not because you were caught, not because the walls were closing in, but because you decided that the man you want to be does not let the people he loves live inside a lie. That conversation will be one of the hardest you have ever had.

It will not go smoothly. It will not produce immediate resolution or gratitude or relief. But it will be the first honest thing you have done in this situation. And it will be yours — not something that happened to you, but something you chose. That distinction matters more than you might currently believe. It will matter more to her than you can currently predict. And it will matter most of all to the man you are trying to become.

Whatever stage you are at — mid-explosion, post-explosion, or pre-explosion and hoping to avoid it — the message of this chapter is the same.

Stop managing. Stop calculating. Stop assessing her reaction for proportionality and timing your honesty around it. Stop treating the truth as something to be dispensed in careful doses designed to minimize your own discomfort. Stop doing what you have always done, which is to take the information she needs to understand her own life and decide, unilaterally, how much of it she gets and when.

Give her the whole truth. All of it, as completely and as carefully as you can, as quickly as you can get yourself to do it. Not because it will make things easy — it will not. Not because it guarantees a particular outcome — it does not. But because it is the only foundation on which anything real can be rebuilt. And because she is a person, not a project. She deserves to know the reality of the life she is living. She has always deserved that. You just have not been giving it to her.

The explosion is not the end. For the man willing to do what comes next, it is the beginning. The most painful possible beginning, the one with the worst starting conditions and the longest road ahead. But a real beginning. The first honest ground you have stood on in longer than you probably want to admit.

Stand on it. Stay on it. What comes next will tell you what you are made of.

PART 4

THE TURN

CHAPTER 9

THE DECISION THAT CHANGES EVERYTHING

Everything we have covered in this book up to this point has been about understanding. Understanding the neuroscience of the lying habit. Understanding the web you built and what it cost you to maintain it. Understanding the mask, the self-deception, the roots that run back into boyhood and culture and the specific wounds of the life you lived before you arrived in this marriage. Understanding what the lying has been costing you and the people you love, and what the explosion looks like when the structure finally comes down.

Understanding matters. It is not optional, and I would not have spent eight chapters on it if it were. But here is what understanding, by itself, cannot do. It cannot change anything. A man can understand every mechanism of his deception with complete clarity and still lie tomorrow morning before breakfast. Knowledge about a pattern is not the same as breaking the pattern. Insight is the beginning of the road, not the destination.

What actually changes things is a decision. Not a resolution — resolutions are soft, they are made in moments of emotion and forgotten when the emotion passes. Not an intention — intentions are what men have when they want to change without committing to the cost of it. A decision. The kind that settles into your bones and stays there. The kind that reorients everything that follows, not because it makes the path easy but because it makes the direction clear.

This chapter is about that decision. What it actually looks like. What it actually requires. And why it is the only thing that makes any of what follows possible.

I have been in the room when men make this decision, and I can tell you that it does not always look the way you might expect. It is rarely a dramatic moment. It is rarely a single conversation that crystallizes everything. Sometimes it's a quiet Tuesday morning when a man sits alone with his coffee and something shifts—a sudden clarity, a settling, a sense that he's finally stopped running from what's been chasing him for years. Other times it happens in a coaching session, not in the moment of insight, but in the silence that follows—when he grows still, and you can see something change in his face. Not quite emotion, but something deeper—like a decision forming beneath the surface of feeling.

What I have noticed consistently, across many years and many men, is that the real decision is almost never about the marriage. The man who decides to stop lying because he wants to save the marriage has made a tactical calculation, not a fundamental choice. He has decided that honesty is the best current strategy for achieving a desired outcome. And when honesty stops feeling strategic — when it gets harder than he anticipated, when it produces responses he did not expect, when the path to saving the marriage looks longer and more uncertain than he was prepared for — that kind of decision will not hold.

The decision that holds is the one about who the man is going to be. Not about the marriage. Not about the consequences. About identity. About the kind of man he is willing to become, regardless of what that becoming costs him, regardless of what outcome it produces, regardless of whether the people around him respond to it the way he hopes they will. That decision sounds simple. It is the hardest thing most men will ever do.

I want to tell you about a man named Solomon, because his story illustrates what this decision looks like in practice and what it costs to make it and hold it. Solomon was forty-one when I first worked with him. He was a man of significant professional accomplishment and considerable personal wreckage — two failed businesses, a bankruptcy he had concealed from his current wife, a pattern of financial deception that had been running since before they married, and an emotional unavailability that had slowly made the marriage a polite and functional shell.

Solomon came to coaching not because he had been discovered but because he had developed, over the preceding months, what he described as an inability to sleep. He would lie awake for hours, not anxious in an identifiable way, not cycling through worries he could name, just awake. Present in the dark in a way that felt, he said, almost punishing. As if some part of him had decided it was time to pay attention and was refusing to be put off any longer.

We worked together for several months before Solomon made what I am calling the decision. I could see it building for weeks before it arrived. He was getting closer to something uncomfortable — not the facts of what he had done, which he had disclosed fairly early, but the deeper question of what those facts meant about who he was and who he was willing to be going forward. That question kept presenting itself and he kept finding ways around it, ways to stay in the realm of analysis and explanation rather than arriving at the place where a choice had to be made.

Then one day he came in and he was different. Not dramatically different. Quieter, maybe. There was a stillness to him that had not been there before. He sat down and said: "I've decided I'm going to tell her everything. Not because I think it will save the marriage. I don't know if it will. But because I have been lying to her since before we got married, and she has built her life on something that isn't real, and I cannot be the kind of man who lets that continue. Whatever happens after, that's what I have to do."

That is the decision. Not "I am going to try to be more honest." Not "I am going to work on this." A clear, grounded, outcome-independent commitment to a different way of being. I am going to tell her everything. I do not know what that produces. I know it is what I have to do.

Solomon told his wife everything over the course of three conversations across a single week. It was, by his account, the worst week of his life. She was devastated. She was furious. She asked him to leave the house for a period of time, and he did.

He did not perform contrition or manage her reaction or attempt to accelerate the timeline of her processing. He simply stayed honest, stayed available, and waited. The marriage did not immediately survive. It went through an extended period of separation and uncertainty that lasted the better part of a year. But Solomon himself — as a man, as a person with an interior life he could actually inhabit — was transformed by that week in ways that have proved permanent.

He told me later: "I didn't know I was suffocating until I could breathe. I didn't know how much of myself I had given away to the lying until I stopped lying and found out there was a self left." The marriage eventually reconciled. But Solomon does not describe the reconciliation as the meaningful outcome. He describes the decision as the meaningful outcome. The marriage surviving was a consequence. The decision was the thing.

I want to spend some time on what radical honesty actually means, because the phrase gets used in ways that range from genuinely useful to frankly destructive, and the distinction matters enormously.

Radical honesty, as I use the term in coaching, does not mean saying every thought that passes through your mind without filter. It does not mean brutal candor deployed without regard for impact. It does not mean confessing every fleeting feeling or desire or doubt as a way of performing transparency. There is a version of radical honesty that is actually a sophisticated form of self-indulgence — a man unloading his interior life onto his partner without consideration for the difference between what is relevant and what is simply unprocessed noise. That is not what we are talking about.

What we are talking about is this: no more constructed realities. No more managed versions. No more strategic omissions. No more decisions, made unilaterally, about what your wife is permitted to know about the life she is living. Full disclosure on anything that materially affects her understanding of her own situation, her own relationship, her own choices. And from that foundation of full disclosure, going forward, a commitment to honesty that is not conditional on whether the truth is convenient, comfortable, or likely to produce the response you are hoping for.

Radical honesty means that when something is true, you say it. When you do not know something, you say that instead of constructing confidence you do not have. When you have made a mistake, you name it before someone finds it. When you are struggling — financially, emotionally, professionally, relationally — you say so, because your wife is your partner and partners are supposed to navigate the hard things together rather than managing each other's perception of whether there are any hard things at all.

This level of honesty will feel, at first, almost physically uncomfortable. If you have been managing your self-presentation for years, genuine transparency will feel like standing in a room with no walls. Exposed. Vulnerable in a way that your entire psychological history has trained you to avoid. That discomfort is not a sign that you are doing it wrong. It is a sign that you are doing something new, and new things feel strange before they feel natural. The discomfort is the old wiring complaining. Stay with it. The complaining settles.

There is a question I get asked regularly by men who are at this turning point, and I want to address it directly because dodging it would be a disservice. The question is: what if I tell the truth and she leaves? It is a real question. It deserves a real answer, not a reassurance.

She might leave. Honesty does not guarantee a particular outcome. Some marriages do not survive the full truth. Some relationships have been damaged past the point where even genuine change and genuine transparency can rebuild them, because trust, once broken in certain ways and to certain depths, does not always reconstitute. That is a reality and pretending otherwise would be its own form of deception.

But here is what I need you to understand about that possibility. A marriage maintained by deception is not actually a marriage. It is a performance of a marriage — a set of behaviors and structures and commitments that exist in a space where the fundamental requirement of genuine partnership, which is honest presence, has been removed. You cannot lose something you do not actually have. What you would lose, if the truth ends the marriage, is the performance. What you would gain — what you cannot have as long as the performance is running — is yourself.

And a man who has himself — who knows who he is, who is not divided, who is not managing and performing and calculating — is capable of something the man inside the deception is not. He is capable of an actual relationship. Whether that relationship is with this wife, or in a different configuration after the marriage has ended, or alone for a period while he becomes someone worth being with — he is capable of something real. The man inside the deception is not. He can only maintain what he has, which is false, or lose what he never truly had. Neither of those is a life. They are just two different versions of the same limitation.

Tell the truth. Whatever it costs. Tell it because you are a man, not because you have calculated that it is strategically optimal. Tell it because the people who love you deserve to love the real version of you. Tell it because you deserve to be known. Tell it because you have been living in a house built on sand and you are finally tired of watching it shift under your feet every time the weather changes. Tell it because you cannot tell me, looking honestly at the life you have been living, that it has been worth it.

Let me say something about the relationship between decision and behavior, because this is where a lot of men get tripped up. They make the decision — genuinely, in the way I have described, bone-deep and outcome-independent — and then they expect the behavior to immediately follow. And sometimes it does. But often it does not, because the neural pathways we talked about in chapter two do not dissolve overnight just because a man has decided to stop running them. The decision is real and it matters enormously, but it does not instantly rewire a brain that has been practicing deception for years.

This means that after the decision, there will be moments — particularly in high-stress situations, in moments of conflict or vulnerability — where the old instinct fires before the new commitment catches up. You will start to manage, to omit, to reach for the safer version, before the part of you that has decided differently intervenes. This is not a sign that the decision was false. It is a sign that you are human and that change is a process rather than an event. What matters is what you do in the moment after the instinct fires. Whether you let it run, or whether you catch it, name it, and correct it.

That catching and correcting is itself an act of honesty. "I just started to minimize that and I want to say it again more accurately." "I realized I left something out and I need to add it." "I told you I was fine and I wasn't, and I don't want to do that anymore." These are not defeats. These are evidence of the decision in practice. They are what it looks like to be a man who is changing rather than a man who is performing having changed. The distinction will matter more to her than you know. It will matter more to you, in time, than you can currently imagine.

The decision is not a destination. It is a direction. You do not arrive at honesty and then relax into it. You practice it, daily, in the small moments where it would be easier to omit or deflect or simplify. You practice it in the big moments where the stakes are high enough that every instinct is screaming at you to manage. You practice it when she asks a question that makes you want to breathe carefully before you answer. You practice it when things are going well and the temptation to leave a complicated truth unsaid is not fear but simple comfort.

You practice it until it is no longer practice. Until the honest response is the one that comes first, that feels most natural, that requires the least effort. Until the wiring has been rebuilt in a different direction. Until the man you decided to be and the man you actually are have, for the first time in a long time, become the same man.

That convergence is what we are building toward. Not the absence of difficulty — an honest life is not a frictionless one. Not the guarantee of a particular outcome — honesty is not a transaction, it is a value. But the convergence of the interior and the exterior. The experience of moving through your own life as a single, coherent, undivided person. The particular freedom that belongs only to the man who has nothing to hide.

Make the decision. Not for her. Not for the marriage. Not because this book told you to. Because somewhere underneath all of the performance and the protection and the years of careful management, there is a man who knows that this is not who he was supposed to become. And that man deserves a chance to find out what he is actually capable of.

Give him that chance. Decide.

CHAPTER 10

HOW TO ACTUALLY STOP: PRACTICAL STEPS THAT WORK

We have spent nine chapters building the foundation for this one. We have looked at what lying is, where it comes from, what it costs, and what the decision to stop actually means at the level of identity. If you have read everything up to this point and sat honestly with what it asked of you, you are not the same man who opened this book. Something has shifted — not completely, not permanently yet, but enough. Enough to be ready for the work that this chapter contains.

Because this chapter is work. Not reflection. Not more understanding. Practical, concrete, daily work — the kind that does not feel significant in any single instance but that compounds over time into something that genuinely changes the structure of your interior life. The neuroscience we covered in chapter two tells us that the brain rewires itself through repetition. What you repeat becomes who you are. So this chapter is about what to repeat. What to practice. What to build, day by day, until the honest response is the one that arrives first and the lying instinct is the one that has to catch up.

Let me be direct about what this chapter is not. It is not a list of tips. It is not a quick fix. It is not a set of techniques that work from the outside in

— that change your behavior while leaving the interior untouched. Everything here is designed to work from the inside out, which means it requires more than reading. It requires doing. And doing it when you do not feel like it. And doing it again when you slip. And understanding that slipping is not failure but data — information about where the old wiring is still strong and where the new wiring needs more reinforcement.

The first and most foundational practice is trigger mapping. A trigger, in the context of the lying habit, is any situation, emotion, or conversational dynamic that reliably produces the impulse to deceive. Not the lie itself — the impulse. The moment right before the lie where something in your nervous system signals danger and reaches for the familiar solution. Your triggers are specific to you, shaped by your history and your particular patterns, but there are categories that appear consistently across the men I work with.

Conflict is one of the most common. The moment a conversation starts to feel like it might become difficult, the lying instinct fires — a preemptive reach for the version of reality that keeps the difficulty from arriving.

Questions about whereabouts, about money, about the state of your emotional life, about things you have done that you know she would find troubling — these questions have been triggering the managed response for so long that the trigger-to-lie pathway is extremely well established. You barely register the question before the shaped answer is already forming.

Shame is another. Anything that activates the fear of being seen as inadequate, as failing, as not being the man you are supposed to be. Financial problems. Professional struggles. Mistakes you have made. Feelings you have that contradict the image. Shame fires and the instinct is to conceal, to manage, to present the version of the situation that preserves the image of competence and control.

A third trigger is what I call perceived threat to access — the sense that honesty will cost you something you are not ready to give up. The relationship outside the marriage. The habit you have been hiding. The pattern of behavior that you know is problematic but have not yet been willing to address. When a conversation approaches the perimeter of that thing, the lying instinct activates not just to protect the secret but to protect your continued access to it.

Your work is to map your specific triggers with as much precision as you can. Not in the abstract, but in the particular. Which conversations make you reach for the managed version? Which emotions precede the impulse to omit or deflect? Which topics make you feel the familiar tightening in your chest that tells you the lying instinct is about to run? Write them down. Name them. Not because naming them makes them disappear, but because a trigger you can see is a trigger you have a chance of catching before it runs. The ones that stay unnamed are the ones that keep running your behavior without your awareness or your consent.

The second practice is what I call the pause and the window. This comes directly from cognitive behavioral therapy and from mindfulness-based interventions, and it is the most consistently effective tool I have seen in coaching work with men who are working to break the lying habit.

The pause is exactly what it sounds like. When you feel the trigger fire — when you sense the conversation moving toward territory that has historically produced the managed response — you pause before you speak. Not for long. A breath. Two seconds. Enough to create what researchers call the window of space between stimulus and response.

The space where choice lives. Without the pause, the habit runs automatically. With it, there is a moment — small, sometimes painfully small — where you can intervene. Where the conscious, decision-making part of your brain has a chance to catch up with the instinct and redirect it.

In that window, you ask yourself one question. Not a complex question. A single, simple one: is what I am about to say true? Not entirely true. Not true enough. True. If the answer is yes, say it. If the answer is no, or not entirely, or I am about to leave something significant out, then you are standing at the precise moment where the decision gets made real. Not in the abstract. Not in principle. Right here, in this conversation, in this sentence, with this person.

The window practice sounds deceptively simple. It is not simple. In the early stages of building it, when the lying habit is strong and the honest response is still unfamiliar and uncomfortable, two seconds will feel inadequate. The managed version will come out anyway, sometimes before the window fully opens.

When that happens — and it will happen — you do not write off the attempt. You catch it. You say: I just said that, and it was not entirely accurate. What I should have said is this. The correction is the practice. The willingness to correct, even after the lie has already left your mouth, is what reinforces the new pathway and weakens the old one.

The third practice is honesty in low stakes situations. This is one of the most underestimated tools available to a man who is trying to rebuild his relationship with truth, and it is the one most men skip because it does not feel significant enough to bother with.

Here is what the research on habit change tells us: new behaviors are most effectively established in conditions of low threat, where the cost of getting it wrong is minimal and the reward of getting it right is immediately felt. The high-stakes truth — the disclosure of the affair, the admission of the financial disaster, the full accounting of the years of deception — is necessary and it must happen.

But it is a terrible environment for building a new habit. The stakes are too high, the emotions too intense, the old instincts too loud. Attempting to rewire the lying habit exclusively in high-stakes situations is like trying to learn to swim in deep water with no instruction. You might survive it. You are unlikely to learn good form.

Low-stakes honesty is the pool with the shallow end. The practice of saying true things in situations where the consequences are manageable. When she asks how your day was and the true answer is that it was difficult and you feel like you are falling behind, say that instead of fine. When she asks if you like the dinner and the honest answer is that it is not your favorite, say that with kindness instead of performing enthusiasm you do not feel. When she makes a plan that does not appeal to you, say so clearly and honestly rather than agreeing and then building quiet resentment around the agreement.

These feel like small things. They are small things. But they are the daily repetitions that rebuild the wiring. Every time you choose the honest response in a low-stakes situation, you are laying down another strand of the new pathway. You are making the honest response slightly more familiar, slightly less threatening, slightly more available the next time. And over weeks and months of consistent practice, those small repetitions accumulate into something that begins to feel like a different relationship with the truth — one where honesty is the default rather than the effortful exception.

The fourth practice is the daily honesty audit. This is a journaling practice, and I will tell you in advance that many of the men I work with resist it initially because they associate journaling with self-indulgence or because they do not think of themselves as writers or because the idea of sitting alone with their interior life on paper feels uncomfortable in ways they cannot quite articulate. That discomfort is useful information. The discomfort of turning toward your interior life honestly, in a space where there is no audience and no management necessary, is exactly the discomfort that the practice is designed to build tolerance for.

The audit is simple. At the end of each day — in the evening, before bed, whenever you can give it ten uninterrupted minutes — you review the day and answer three questions. Where did I tell the truth today? Where did I not tell the truth, fully or partially? What was I protecting when I chose the incomplete version?

That third question is the one that matters most. It is the one that keeps the work connected to the root rather than staying on the surface of behavior. You are not just cataloguing lies. You are tracing each one back to the fear or the shame or the comfort or the access that it was serving. You are keeping visible, day by day, the inventory of what the lying habit is still protecting, so that you can make deliberate choices about whether those things are actually worth protecting or whether they are relics of a way of operating that you have decided to leave behind.

Over time, the audit does something else. It creates a record of progress that is invisible without it. The man who is three months into this work and feeling discouraged because change feels slow can look back at his journal and see the entries from the first week — see how many omissions and managed responses he was logging, how close together the triggers were firing, how unfamiliar the honest response felt. And he can see how that has shifted. The audit makes the invisible progress visible, which matters enormously in the middle of a process that rarely produces the dramatic external results that would otherwise confirm that something is changing.

The fifth practice addresses one of the most specific and most damaging forms of dishonesty that men in marriages engage in, and it is the one that is easiest to overlook because it does not feel like lying. It is lying by omission, and it requires its own direct and deliberate attention.

Lying by omission is the leaving out of information that your partner would want and need to have in order to accurately understand the situation she is in. It does not require an active false statement. It requires only that you allow a false impression to persist by withholding the information that would correct it.

Men who have committed to stopping outright deception very often continue omitting, because the internal logic feels different — I did not lie, I just did not mention it. But the effect is identical. She is operating on an incomplete and therefore inaccurate picture of reality. And you are the one who has the information that would complete it and has chosen, for whatever reason, not to share it.

The practice here is to develop the habit of asking yourself, in any significant conversation, what am I not saying? Not what might I be lying about. What am I not saying that is relevant? What am I leaving in the space between sentences that belongs in the conversation?

This question is uncomfortable precisely because the omissions often feel justifiable — the information is complicated, or the timing feels wrong, or you are not sure how to frame it, or you have told yourself that this particular detail does not rise to the level of requiring disclosure. These are the same justifications that built the web. Do not let them rebuild it quietly under cover of the more obvious work.

A useful rule of thumb: if you would be uncomfortable having her find out that you knew something and did not tell her, you should tell her. Not because this rule eliminates all ambiguity — it does not — but because the discomfort test is usually an accurate read on whether the omission is genuinely irrelevant or whether it is the kind of strategic silence that has always been part of the problem.

The sixth practice is what I call the correction without collapse. This is for the moments — and they will come — when you have lied or omitted and you realize it, whether in the moment or minutes or hours later. The old response to these moments is either to let it go and hope it does not matter, or to spiral into guilt and self-condemnation that is more about managing your own emotional state than about actually addressing the dishonesty. Neither of those serves the work.

The correction without collapse is exactly what it sounds like. You catch the lie or the omission. You go back. You say: I told you X, and that was not entirely accurate. What I should have said is Y. You do not perform elaborate apologies.

You do not spiral into a lengthy explanation of your psychological history and the childhood roots of the dishonesty and how hard you are working to change. You correct the record, clearly and directly, without making the correction into a drama that centers your own emotional experience rather than the simple act of getting the truth into the room.

This practice is important for two reasons. First, the obvious one: it keeps the record accurate and prevents small omissions and managed responses from accumulating into something larger. Second, and less obvious: it reinforces the identity shift rather than undermining it.

The man who catches his own dishonesty and corrects it, without prompting and without drama, is demonstrating — to her and to himself — that he is the kind of person who values truth enough to be uncomfortable in its service. That demonstration, repeated over time, is the actual evidence of change. Not the announcement that you have changed. The behavior.

One more thing before I close this chapter, because it is the thing that ties all of these practices together and gives them their deeper purpose. The practices I have described are not techniques for appearing more honest. They are disciplines for becoming more honest. The distinction is everything.

A man who is using these tools to perform trustworthiness for an audience is still, at the root, doing what he has always done — managing his presentation rather than changing his nature. The tools will not work that way. Or more precisely, they will appear to work — the behavior will change, the external patterns will shift — but the interior will remain divided and the pressure of that division will eventually find another expression.

The practices work when they are in service of the decision we talked about in chapter nine. When they are expressions of the commitment to be a particular kind of man, rather than instruments in the service of a particular outcome. Trigger mapping, the pause and the window, low-stakes honesty, the daily audit, the omission check, the correction without collapse — these are the daily practices of a man who has decided to live without concealment. Not the techniques of a man who is trying to look like he has decided.

You will know the difference. So will she. And in time, if you do this honestly and consistently and without the constant calculation of what it is producing, the man you are practicing being will become the man you actually are. The gap will close. Not all at once. Not without setback and frustration and moments where the old instinct wins and you have to correct and start again. But it will close.

That closing is what the rest of your life depends on. Not the techniques. The decision they are in service of. Stay connected to that, and the work will hold. Do the work.

CHAPTER 11

ACCOUNTABILITY: WHY YOU CANNOT DO THIS ALONE

There is a particular kind of stubbornness in men who are trying to change. It is not always obvious, because it does not look like resistance. It looks like self-sufficiency. It looks like taking responsibility, handling your own problems, not burdening other people with the mess you made. It looks, from the outside and sometimes even from the inside, like strength. And it is one of the most reliable ways to fail at this work that I have ever encountered.

The man who decides to stop lying and then attempts to execute that decision entirely alone, inside his own head, with only his own judgment as a check on his own behavior, has not fully understood what he is up against. He is using the same instrument that built the problem to try to fix it. He is trusting a mind that has demonstrated, repeatedly and over years, that it is capable of sophisticated self-deception — of believing its own justifications, of editing its own record, of concluding that it is being honest when it is still managing. That mind is not a reliable auditor of its own integrity. No mind is. That is not a criticism. It is a structural limitation of being human.

This chapter is about accountability — what it is, what it is not, why it is not optional, and how to build it in ways that actually work. Not the surveillance version of accountability, which does not work and which is about control rather than growth. The real version, which is about relationship — about being known by someone outside your own head who can see you clearly enough to call you on what you cannot see yourself.

Let me start with why isolation is the natural habitat of the lying man, because understanding that makes the importance of breaking the isolation clearer. Deception requires secrecy. Secrecy requires privacy. And privacy, over years of living inside a managed reality, becomes a deeply ingrained operating mode. The man who has been keeping significant secrets does not just keep those specific secrets — he develops a general orientation toward concealment, a reflexive withholding that extends beyond the actual hidden things into his whole relationship with vulnerability and disclosure.

He becomes a man who handles things internally. Who does not ask for help, not because help is unavailable but because asking for it requires showing someone the real situation, and showing someone the real situation requires admitting that the real situation is what it is. He becomes a man whose friendships, such as they are, stay at the surface — conversations about work and sports and shared history, but never about the interior of his life, never about the things that are actually happening underneath the presentation he maintains. He becomes, over time, genuinely alone in the way that matters most, even when he is surrounded by people who care about him.

That isolation is not incidental to the lying. It is structural. The lie requires it. The secrecy requires it. And when the man decides to stop lying, the isolation does not automatically lift. It has to be actively dismantled, deliberately and with some difficulty, because the habits of concealment do not disappear just because the decision to stop has been made. Isolation is what the lying built as its home. And you cannot do the work of dismantling the lying while still living in its home.

Proverbs 27:17 says: as iron sharpens iron, so one person sharpens another. It is a spare and practical image — two pieces of metal, friction between them, each one made more precise and more useful by the contact with the other. Not softened. Sharpened. The metaphor does not promise comfort. It promises clarity. The kind of clarity that only comes from genuine contact with another person who is willing to tell you the truth about what they see.

That is what real accountability is. Not someone monitoring your behavior from a position of suspicion. Not a warden with a checklist. A person — or in the best case, a small number of people — who knows the real situation, who has agreed to engage with you honestly about your progress and your failures, and whose relationship with you is strong enough to survive the truth being said in both directions. A person who will not let you minimize what you have done. Who will not let you stay comfortable when comfort is not what serves you. Who will ask the question you are hoping no one asks, because they care more about your actual growth than they do about maintaining a pleasant dynamic between you.

That kind of relationship does not emerge automatically. It has to be chosen and cultivated. And choosing it requires something that the isolation of the lying life has made unfamiliar: the willingness to be genuinely known by another person. To show them the actual situation, not the managed version. To say out loud, to a face you have to look at, the things you have only ever permitted yourself to think in private. That act of disclosure — not to your wife, not as a formal confession, but to another person who can hold it without being destroyed by it — is often the first real experience of transparency that men in this process have. And it is often transformative in ways they did not anticipate.

Let me talk practically about what an accountability relationship looks like, because the word accountability gets used loosely and it helps to be specific about what you are actually building.

The accountability partner in this context is someone who knows enough of the truth about your situation to be useful. Not someone you have told a comfortable summary. Someone who knows the actual shape of what you have been doing and what you are working to change.

Without that foundation, the relationship cannot function as accountability — it can only function as another audience for the managed version, which is precisely what you are trying to stop performing.

This person should be someone whose judgment you respect, whose own life demonstrates the kind of integrity you are working toward, and who has enough maturity and emotional stability to engage with your situation without either collapsing into sympathy that lets you off the hook or hardening into judgment that makes honesty feel unsafe. That combination is rarer than it sounds, which is why the choice of an accountability partner deserves real care and real thought rather than defaulting to whoever is most conveniently available.

The relationship works through regular, honest contact — not just when you have slipped or are in crisis, but as a consistent and scheduled presence in your week. A conversation, a check-in, a commitment to show up with your actual interior rather than your best presentation. The regularity matters because the lying habit is regular.

It fires daily, in small moments as well as large ones. An accountability relationship that only activates in moments of obvious crisis is not robust enough to address what needs addressing. It needs to be woven into the ordinary fabric of your week, so that the ordinary moments — the small omissions, the low-stakes deflections, the automatic reaches for the managed version — are being seen and named and worked with, not just the catastrophic ones.

I want to say something about therapy and professional support, because there are men who will read this chapter and decide that what I am describing is therapy, and who will either embrace that or resist it depending on their history with the idea. Let me be direct: for many men doing this work, professional therapeutic support is not just useful. It is necessary. Not because the work cannot happen without it, but because the roots of the lying pattern — the childhood conditioning, the attachment wounds, the shame architecture, the specific traumas that may have shaped the particular form your deception took — are often deep enough to require a trained professional to help excavate them safely.

A therapist who specializes in men's work, in couples recovery, in addiction and compulsive behavior, or in the specific patterns of deception that show up in marital infidelity brings tools and frameworks that a well-intentioned accountability partner cannot provide. They can help you understand the specific mechanisms of your pattern at a level of depth and precision that self-reflection alone cannot reach. They can hold the work in a container that is stable enough to process genuinely difficult material without destabilizing your ability to function in the rest of your life. And they can track your progress over time with a clarity that is difficult to maintain when you are inside the process.

The resistance to therapy among men who need it is well documented and almost entirely driven by the same cultural conditioning we discussed in chapter six — the belief that needing professional help is a sign of inadequacy, that a real man handles his own interior life without outside assistance, that the therapy room is for other people and other problems. That belief is a casualty of the same culture that taught you to hide your struggles in the first place. It is the voice of the mask, trying to stay on. Let it go. Therapy is not weakness. It is the decision to take your interior life seriously enough to bring skilled help to bear on it. That is not failure. That is exactly the kind of self-respect this book has been building toward.

There is also the question of support groups, which deserve mention because they offer something that neither a one-to-one accountability relationship nor individual therapy can fully provide: the experience of being in a room with other men who are doing the same work. Men who have made the same mistakes, told themselves the same justifications, felt the same shame, and are navigating the same difficult path back to integrity.

There is something that happens in those rooms that is difficult to replicate elsewhere. When a man hears another man describe the interior experience of sustained deception — the compartmentalization, the cognitive load, the strange combination of control and terror, the exhaustion of the double life — and recognizes it completely, something in the isolation breaks. He is not alone in this in the way he thought he was. His experience is not unique, not because that diminishes it, but because others have been here and have found a way forward, and their presence in the room is evidence that a way forward exists.

Groups built around infidelity recovery, around sexual compulsivity, around the specific patterns of deception that show up in marital betrayal — these groups exist in most cities and in many online formats. They are not for everyone, and the right fit matters. But for many men, the experience of showing up in a group as the real version of themselves, without the performance and without the management, is one of the most powerful early experiences of what life without concealment can actually feel like. It is practice in the most literal sense — a regular rehearsal of honesty in a context designed to make honesty survivable.

I want to draw a clear line between accountability and surveillance, because the two get conflated in ways that damage both. Accountability is a relationship of mutual respect in which you voluntarily submit your behavior and your interior life to the honest engagement of someone you trust. Surveillance is a system of monitoring imposed from outside, driven by distrust, designed to catch rather than to support.

In the aftermath of discovery, many couples default to a version of surveillance — shared phone access, location tracking, check-in requirements, demands for information that are more about the injured partner's anxiety than about the changing partner's growth. I understand why this happens. The betrayed partner's nervous system is in a state of genuine threat, and the monitoring behaviors are an attempt to create a sense of control in a situation that has been revealed as deeply out of control. That makes complete human sense.

But surveillance, as the primary accountability mechanism, does not produce trustworthiness. It produces behavior modification in the presence of monitoring, which is not the same thing. A man who is honest because he knows his phone is being checked is not practicing honesty. He is practicing not getting caught, which is precisely what he was always practicing. The behavior looks the same from the outside. The interior is unchanged. And the moment the monitoring relaxes, the behavior that monitoring was suppressing has a clear path to return, because nothing inside the man has actually shifted.

Real accountability produces trustworthiness that persists in the absence of monitoring. The man who is honest in the moments when no one is checking — when he could omit without anyone knowing, when he could manage the version and face no consequence — is the man who is actually changing. That man is produced not by surveillance but by the genuine interior shift that comes from decision, from daily practice, and from the kind of accountability relationship that engages with who he is rather than just tracking what he does.

If your wife needs a period of increased transparency — access to your phone, check-ins, more information than she previously had about your whereabouts and activities — give it to her willingly and without resentment. Not as reluctant compliance, not as a calculated demonstration of your cooperation, but as a genuine acknowledgment that you have destroyed her ability to trust her own read on your behavior and that rebuilding that trust requires making yourself more legible, not less, for as long as she needs that. That is not surveillance you are submitting to. That is reparation you are offering. There is a meaningful difference in how you hold it, and she will feel which one it is.

I want to close this chapter by talking about what genuine accountability ultimately produces, because the men who do this work well — who build real accountability relationships and maintain them and show up honestly in them over time — describe something that goes beyond the specific goal of stopping the lying. They describe a different experience of being a man.

For most of their adult lives, they have operated inside a version of aloneness that they did not always have a name for. Not loneliness in the social sense — they had people around them, relationships, friendships, a family. But alone in the interior sense. Alone with the parts of themselves they could not show anyone. Alone with the knowledge of what they were doing and why and what it was costing. Alone in the specific way that the man who is managing his presentation is always alone, because the management creates a permanent distance between himself and everyone he is managing for.

When that aloneness breaks — when a man finally shows up, fully and honestly, in a relationship that can hold the real version of him and does not collapse or condemn — something happens that is difficult to describe without sounding overstated but that every man who has experienced it will recognize immediately. It is the experience of being known. Of being seen clearly and completely, and found acceptable — not despite the real situation, but with full knowledge of it. That experience, which may seem like a small thing from the outside, is often the most significant thing a man in this process encounters. Because it answers the question that the deception was built to prevent from ever being tested.

The question was: if anyone knew the real version of me, would they stay? The deception was built to keep that question from ever getting an answer. The accountability relationship is the first place where the man tests it, in a context designed to make the testing survivable. And he discovers that the answer is not always no. That the real version of him, brought into the light and held honestly, is not the unacceptable thing he spent years hiding. It is a man with wounds and failures and a pattern he is working to change. And that man, it turns out, is someone people can know and choose to stand beside.

That discovery does not fix everything. It does not repair the marriage by itself or undo the damage that has been done or make the hard work ahead any less hard. But it changes what the man believes is possible. It breaks the foundational lie that drove everything else — the lie that he was too damaged to be known, that concealment was his only protection, that the real version of him could not survive contact with another person's honest awareness.

It can survive. It does survive. And in surviving it, the man begins to understand something that all the successful deception in the world never gave him and never could. He is not alone. He never had to be.

CHAPTER 12

THE MAN YOU WERE ALWAYS SUPPOSED TO BE

I want you to think about your funeral. Not morbidly. Not as an exercise in dread. But as a lens — the clearest one available to a man who wants to understand what his life is actually for and whether the way he is currently living it is pointed in the right direction. Think about who will be in that room. Your wife, if the marriage survives. Your children, who will be adults by then, carrying in their bodies and their relationships everything they absorbed from watching you live. Your friends, the ones who knew you across the arc of your life. And think about what they will say.

Not what they will say in the formal remarks — eulogies are often generous beyond accuracy. What they will say to each other quietly, in the parking lot afterward, in the honest conversation that happens when the ceremony is over and the performance of grief has given way to the real one. What they will say when someone asks what kind of man he was. What they will remember as the defining quality of your presence in their lives. What they will feel in their bodies when they think about what it meant to be known by you, loved by you, raised by you, married to you.

Hold that image for a moment. Hold it honestly, without the softening filter of how you would like it to look. And then ask yourself the question that every man who has sat in my coaching room has eventually had to ask: is the man I am becoming the man I want to be remembered as?

Here is what I have seen, in room after room, when men finally get honest about the answer to that question. Most of them know — have always known, somewhere below the level of comfortable awareness — exactly who they are capable of being. They have a sense of it, a felt intuition of the man they could be if they stopped managing and protecting and performing. They have caught glimpses of him in moments of genuine connection, in the rare conversations where the mask slipped and something real passed between them and another person and the world did not end. They know he is in there. They have just spent years, sometimes decades, making choices that moved them further from him rather than closer.

The work of this book — all twelve chapters of it — has been about closing that distance. About understanding what created it, what it costs to maintain it, and what it takes to finally begin moving in the other direction. We have not been talking about becoming someone new. We have been talking about returning to something true. The man underneath the mask, the man behind the performance, the man who existed before the lying became habitual and the hiding became home — that man is not a fantasy. He is the most real version of you there is. And everything we have discussed has been in service of finding our way back to him.

Let me describe what that man looks like. Not as an abstraction, not as a distant aspiration, but in the specific and daily texture of what his life actually feels like from the inside.

He wakes up in the morning without the first thought being a calculation. He does not open his eyes and immediately begin reviewing the current state of his deceptions, checking for inconsistencies, assessing what the day might bring in the way of risk. He wakes up and the morning is simply the morning — his wife beside him, the particular quality of light through the window, the ordinary sounds of the household coming to life. He is present in it. Not performing presence. Actually there.

He moves through his day without the background hum of hypervigilance that has been the soundtrack of the lying life. He has conversations without calculating what to reveal and what to withhold. He answers questions directly because the direct answer is also the honest one and there is no longer a gap between those two things that requires management. He can look the people he loves in the eye without the particular kind of difficulty that comes from knowing that the person looking back at you does not have the full picture.

When things go wrong — and they do, because an honest life is not a frictionless one — he says so. When he is struggling, he names it. When he has made a mistake, he owns it before someone finds it. He has learned, through practice that was initially painful and is now simply second nature, that the truth delivered promptly and clearly and without excessive apology is almost always less damaging than the managed version delivered late, under pressure, in pieces. He has learned that the people who love him can handle reality. That he does not need to protect them from it. That the protection he was providing was never for them.

He has a marriage — or whatever the primary intimate relationship of his life has become — that is built on something real. Not on a version of himself he constructed for consumption. On the actual version: imperfect, still growing, capable of failure and honest about it when it happens. His wife knows him. Not the managed presentation, not the edited highlight reel, not the man he decided to let her see. She knows him. And the intimacy of that knowing — the particular depth and warmth that comes from two people who have been genuinely honest with each other over time — is something he never had during the years of deception and something he will not trade away again.

His children see a father who is whole. They may not have the language for it, especially when they are young, but they feel it — the difference between a parent who is fully present and a parent who is somewhere else even when he is physically in the room. They feel the consistency of a man whose inside life and outside life are the same life. They learn, from watching him, that adults can be honest about their struggles and still be competent. That mistakes can be owned rather than hidden. That the people who love each other most tell each other the truth. They are building their template for intimacy from what they observe in him, and what they observe is worth building from.

His friendships — the real ones, the ones with the accountability partners we talked about in the last chapter — have a depth that his previous friendships did not. Not because he found better people. Because he became a better participant. Because he stopped managing his presentation and started showing up as the actual person, which allowed the people around him to stop performing their own versions of okayness and start doing the same. Honesty is contagious in this way. One person who refuses to pretend gives everyone around them a kind of permission. The man who stops lying does not just change his own life. He shifts the emotional temperature of every room he enters.

I want to be honest with you about something, because this is the final chapter and honesty is the point of everything we have done here. The road to becoming this man is not straight. It is not short. It does not begin with a single conversation or a single decision, however important and bone-deep that decision is. It begins there, but it extends through months and years of daily practice, of setback and correction, of moments where the old wiring wins and moments where the new wiring holds and a gradual, mostly invisible shift in who you are and how you move through the world.

There will be days when honesty costs you something significant and the part of you that is still wired for self-protection will look at the cost and ask whether it was worth it. There will be relationships that do not survive your becoming honest, because some relationships were built on the managed version of you and cannot accommodate the real one. There will be a period — sometimes a long one — when you are doing the right things and the people around you are not yet able to believe it, because the evidence of trustworthiness takes time to accumulate and there is no shortcut through that accumulation.

All of that is true. I am not going to soften it for you. But here is what is also true, and what I have watched be true for man after man who has done this work with full commitment and full honesty: the other side of it is a life that is actually yours. Not a performance of a life. Not a managed presentation that requires constant maintenance. Your life, inhabited by the full version of you, lived without the weight of what you have been carrying.

Men who have come through this process describe it in terms that are surprisingly consistent, given how different their stories are. They use the word lighter. They talk about breathing differently. They describe being present in a way they were not before — at dinner, at their children's games, in bed, in the ordinary minutes of an ordinary day. They do not describe a life without difficulty. They describe a life without the particular and suffocating difficulty of being divided, of running two versions of yourself simultaneously, of never being able to fully relax because relaxing means dropping your guard and dropping your guard means the truth might surface.

That difficulty is over for them. And the difficulties that replace it — the honest ones, the ones that come from living a real life in a real relationship with real stakes — are the kind of difficulties that a man can be proud of navigating. They are the difficulties of someone who is present for his own life. That is not a small thing. That is everything.

I want to close by talking about legacy, because it is the largest frame available to us and the one that clarifies everything else.

Every man leaves a legacy. Not just in the formal sense — not just what he accumulated or built or achieved. In the human sense. In the sense of what the people who lived closest to him carry forward into their own lives. What his children absorbed in childhood and carry in their nervous systems as adults. What his wife holds in the deepest places of her understanding of love and partnership. What his friends remember about what it felt like to be known by him. These things outlast everything else. They are passed forward through generations in ways that a man rarely lives long enough to fully see.

The man who lived inside a deception for years, who finally turned toward honesty and did the work of becoming whole — his legacy is not defined by the years of lying. I want you to hear that clearly. Your story is not finished at the worst chapter. The men I have watched do this work, fully and honestly, are not remembered by the people who love them primarily for what they did wrong. They are remembered for the change.

For the moment they stopped running. For the decision they made and the man they became in the years after it. That becoming is what the people closest to them carry forward. That becoming is what shows up in the way their children approach honesty in their own marriages, in the way their wives describe what it means to be truly known by someone, in the texture of every relationship they participated in after they stopped hiding.

You cannot undo what has been done. That is not available, and pretending otherwise would be the last lie this book would tell you. But you can determine what the rest of the story is. You can decide what the people who love you spend the most years of their relationship with you experiencing. You can choose, starting today, to be the man whose legacy is the turn — the man who faced himself honestly and changed, not completely and not without stumbling, but genuinely, in the ways that matter most.

That legacy is available to you. It is not available to the man you have been. It is available to the man you are deciding to become. So here is my final word to you. Not a summary. Not a list of takeaways. A challenge, the same one I give to every man who sits across from me when we reach this point in the work.

Go home tonight and tell the truth about one thing you have not been telling the truth about. Not everything — you do not have to dismantle the entire structure in a single evening, and attempting to do so without the support and preparation this process deserves would be its own kind of mistake. But one thing. One true thing that has been living in the space between you and the person you are supposed to be closest to. One honest statement in the place where a managed one has been sitting.

See what happens. Not to the marriage, not to the conversation, not to her reaction — those things are not yours to control. See what happens to you. See what it feels like to have said a true thing in a place where true things have not been said. See whether the world ends. See whether you are still standing on the other side of it.

You will be. You always were going to be. The catastrophe you have been protecting yourself from has never been as certain as the catastrophe you have been building by continuing to hide. The truth was always survivable. You just had not tested it long enough to know.

Test it now. Keep testing it. Build the practice until the practice builds the man. And let the man you build — honest, present, whole, undivided — be the answer to the question of what kind of person walked through this world and left it better for having been here.

You came to this book because something in you knew that the way you were living was not the way you were meant to live. That knowing was not an accident. It was the most honest part of you, the part that never fully accepted the lie even while you were telling it, trying to get your attention. It has your attention now. Do not waste it.

THE STOP LYING

WORKBOOK

EXERCISES, REFLECTIONS, AND A 30-DAY HONESTY CHALLENGE

This workbook is designed to be used alongside the book. You can work through it chapter by chapter as you read, or read the book in full first and then return here.

Either way works. What does not work is skipping it entirely.

The book gave you understanding. This workbook makes it personal. It asks you to put your specific life, your specific patterns, your specific fears and failures and possibilities on the page where you can see them clearly.

Writing things down does something that reading cannot — it makes the interior exterior, turns the vague into the concrete, and creates a record of where you started and how far you have come.

Use a pen. Write in this book. Make it yours.

PART ONE: CHAPTER REFLECTIONS

For each chapter, answer the questions as honestly as you can. Not the answers that sound right. The true ones.

CHAPTER 1

You Are Not a Bad Man. You Are a Scared One.

1. What is the fear that drives most of your lying? Name it as specifically as you can — not "I was afraid of consequences" but what specific thing you were most afraid of losing or being seen as.

____

____

____

____

2. Think about the last significant lie you told. What were you protecting in that moment? Be honest about whether it was really about her, or really about you.

____

____

____

____

3. Complete this sentence without editing it: "If she knew the full truth about me, I am afraid she would..."

____

____

____

____

4. Where in your life have you felt most like the real version of yourself — not the managed version? What was different about that situation?

____

____

____

____

CHAPTER 2

How Lying Actually Works in Your Brain

1. When did the lying start to feel automatic — like something that happened before you consciously decided to do it? Can you identify the first time it felt effortless?

____

____

____

2. What are the justifications your brain most reliably offers you when you lie? Write them down, the exact internal language. "I lied because..." Write as many as apply.

____

____

____

3. On a scale of 1 to 10, how much do you genuinely believe your own justifications for the lying? What does that number tell you?

____

____

____

4. Derek believed he was an honest person even while running six years of deception. In what ways have you told yourself a similar story about your own character?

____

____

____

CHAPTER 3

The Web You Wove: How One Lie Becomes a Thousand

1. Go back to the first lie — the original one, the strand that started the web. What was it? How old were you in this marriage when you told it? What were you avoiding?

____

____

____

2. How many separate lies are you currently maintaining? Do not estimate vaguely. Try to count. Include omissions.

____

____

____

3. What is the cognitive cost of maintaining your current web? How much mental energy per day goes into tracking, managing, and protecting it?

____

____

____

4. What do you think your wife's intuition is already telling her, even if she has not named it? What does she sense that she cannot prove?

CHAPTER 4

The Man Behind the Mask: Identity and Self-Deception

1. Describe the mask — the version of yourself you present to the world. What does it show? What does it hide?

---

2. How do you square your self-image as a good man with the behavior that contradicts it? Write out the specific justifications you use to hold both things at once.

---

3. If you removed the mask completely — if every person in your life could see the full and unedited version of you — what would they see that they currently do not?

---

4. What would it mean for your daily life to be an integrated man — someone whose inside and outside are the same? What would have to change?

CHAPTER 5

What You're Really Protecting

1. From the list in this chapter — comfort, access, image, options, peace — which one or ones are at the center of your lying? Be specific about what each one means in your particular situation.

---

2. You have told yourself you are lying to protect her. Now tell the truth: what percentage of that protection is actually about protecting yourself? Write the honest number.

---

3. What is the thing the lie is protecting that you are least willing to give up? Name it directly.

---

4. If you gave up that thing — if the lie no longer had anything to protect — what would your life look like? What would open up and what would close?

CHAPTER 6

Where It Started: Secrets, Boyhood, and What You Were Taught

1. What was the atmosphere of honesty in the home you grew up in? Was truth safe? What happened when someone told the truth and it was inconvenient?

2. What did you learn, as a boy, about what men do with their emotional life — their fears, their failures, their doubts? Who taught you that lesson and how?

3. Go back to the earliest memory you have of telling a significant lie. How old were you? What were you afraid would happen if you told the truth?

4. Understanding your history does not excuse the behavior — but it can explain it. What understanding do you have now that the boy who told that first lie did not have?

____

____

____

CHAPTER 7

What It's Actually Costing You

1. Rate the current cost to each of the following on a scale of 1 to 10 — 1 being minimal damage, 10 being severe. Your integrity. Your self-respect. Your marriage. Your children. Your health. Your experience of your own life.

____

____

____

2. Describe in your own words what the "underwater" feeling described in this chapter feels like in your own life. When do you notice it most?

____

____

____

3. What have you missed — genuinely missed, been absent from — because part of your mind was occupied with managing the deception?

____

____

____

4. If the lying continued for ten more years and nothing changed, what would your life look like? Describe it honestly.

____

____

____

CHAPTER 8

The Explosion: What Happens When She Finds Out

1. If you have already been through the explosion: what did you disclose fully and what did you withhold? Looking back, what were you still protecting in that moment?

____

____

____

2. If you have not yet been discovered: what do you believe will happen when the truth comes out? How accurate do you think that prediction is?

____

____

____

3. When her reaction has been painful or intense, have you found yourself shifting focus to how she is handling it rather than what you did to cause it? Be honest.

____

____

____

4. What would it mean for you to choose disclosure before discovery? What is stopping you from doing that today?

CHAPTER 9

The Decision That Changes Everything

1. Have you made the decision — the bone-deep, outcome-independent commitment to becoming an honest man? If yes, describe it in your own words. If not, what is standing between you and it?

2. Is your desire to be honest connected to saving the marriage, or to who you want to be regardless of the outcome? Examine this carefully and answer honestly.

3. What are you most afraid the full truth will cost you? Can you accept that cost in service of the decision?

4. Complete this sentence: "The man I am deciding to become is..."

CHAPTERS 10 & 11

How to Actually Stop / Accountability

1. List your three most consistent lying triggers — the specific situations, emotions, or conversational dynamics that most reliably produce the impulse to deceive.

2. Where in your daily life can you practice low-stakes honesty starting this week? Name three specific situations.

3. Who is the person in your life with the character and discretion to be your accountability partner? What is stopping you from asking them?

____

____

____

____

4. What form of professional support — individual therapy, couples therapy, a men's group — do you need that you have not yet pursued? What is the real reason you have not pursued it?

____

____

____

____

PART TWO: THE LIE INVENTORY

This is the most difficult exercise in the workbook. It is also the most important. The Lie Inventory asks you to list the lies you are currently maintaining — actively or by omission — and to document them honestly on paper. Not for anyone else to read. For you, so that the full shape of what you have built is visible to you rather than existing only as a vague weight you carry. Complete this inventory alone, in a private space, with enough time to do it without rushing. Do not minimize. Do not edit for palatability. The point is not to feel worse about yourself — the point is to see clearly, because you cannot dismantle what you cannot see.

Active Lies — Things You Have Said That Are Not True

For each active lie you are maintaining, write what you told her, what the truth actually is, and what you were protecting when you said it.

Lie 1:

____

____

____

The truth:

____

____

____

What I was protecting:

____

____

____

Lie 2:

____

____

____

The truth:

____

____

____

What I was protecting:

____

____

____

Lie 3:

____

____

____

The truth:

____

____

____

What I was protecting:

____

____

____

Lie 4:

The truth:

What I was protecting:

Lie 5:

The truth:

What I was protecting:

Lies of Omission — Things She Does Not Know That She Should

List the significant omissions — the information you are withholding that would change how she understands her own life if she had it.

Omission 1:

___

___

___

Why I have not told her:

___

___

___

Omission 2:

___

___

___

Why I have not told her:

___

___

___

Omission 3:

___

___

___

Why I have not told her:

____

____

____

The Cost Column

Now go back through everything you wrote above and for each lie or omission, write one specific thing it is costing you right now — not what it might cost in the future, but what it is extracting from your life today.

PART THREE: THE TRIGGER MAP

A trigger is the specific situation, emotion, or conversational dynamic that fires the lying impulse. Use this section to map yours with as much precision as possible. The more specific you are, the more useful this map will be.

My Primary Triggers

Complete each row as specifically as you can. Vague triggers produce vague awareness. Specific triggers can be caught.

Trigger 1 — Describe the specific situation:

____

____

____

The emotion that precedes the lie:

____

____

____

What I typically say or do instead of the truth:

____

____

____

Trigger 2 — Describe the specific situation:

____

____

____

The emotion that precedes the lie:

____

____

____

What I typically say or do instead of the truth:

____

____

____

Trigger 3 — Describe the specific situation:

____

____

____

The emotion that precedes the lie:

____

____

____

What I typically say or do instead of the truth:

____

____

____

Trigger 4 — Describe the specific situation:

____

____

____

The emotion that precedes the lie:

What I typically say or do instead of the truth:

The Honest Response

For each trigger above, write what the honest response would have been. Not the ideal, diplomatic version — the true one. What should you have said?

Trigger 1 — The honest response:

Trigger 2 — The honest response:

Trigger 3 — The honest response:

Trigger 4 — The honest response:

____

____

____

____

PART FOUR: THE TRUTH DECLARATION

The Truth Declaration is a written statement of who you are committing to become. It is not a promise to be perfect. It is not a performance for anyone else.

It is a document between you and yourself — the clearest possible statement of the decision you made in Chapter 9, in your own words, on paper where it cannot be quietly forgotten.

Write it in the first person. Write it in the present tense, as if the man you are becoming is already here. Be specific. Be honest. Be direct.

Read it every morning for the first thirty days. Then read it whenever you feel the old instincts pulling.

My Truth Declaration

I am a man who...

____

____

____

I am no longer a man who...

____

____

____

The people I love deserve...

____

____

____

When I am tempted to lie or omit, I will...

____

____

____

____

The man I am becoming will be remembered for...

____

____

____

____

I make this commitment not to save my marriage or manage a situation, but because...

____

____

____

____

Signed: ________________ Date: ________________

PART FIVE: THE 30-DAY HONESTY CHALLENGE

The 30-Day Honesty Challenge is a daily practice structure. Each day has a specific focus and a brief end-of-day reflection. The goal is not perfection. The goal is consistency — thirty consecutive days of intentional, deliberate practice that begins to lay down new neural pathways and build new patterns of behavior.

Complete each day's reflection in the evening. Keep it brief — three to five minutes. The practice is more important than the reflection. But the reflection keeps the practice honest.

Week One: Awareness

The first week is about seeing the pattern clearly, in real time. You are not trying to change anything yet. You are trying to catch yourself — to notice the trigger, the impulse, and the automatic response, before it has fully run.

Day 1 — Today I noticed the lying impulse fire when:

____

____

____

What I did with it:

____

____

____

Day 2 — The emotion underneath the trigger today was:

____

____

____

What I was protecting:

____

____

____

Day 3 — One thing I said today that was not the full truth:

____

____

____

What the full truth would have been:

____

____

____

Day 4 — One thing I omitted today that should have been said:

____

____

____

What stopped me from saying it:

____

____

____

Day 5 — Where did I use the pause today? Did it work?

____

____

____

Day 6 — Where did I practice low-stakes honesty today?

___

___

___

What happened when I did?

___

___

___

Day 7 — End of Week One. What have I learned about my pattern this week that I did not know clearly before?

___

___

___

Week Two: Practice

This week, you are not just observing. You are intervening. Every time the trigger fires, use the pause. Every time you catch yourself mid-omission, correct it. Every time you choose the honest response over the managed one, note it.

Day 8 — One moment today where I chose honesty over the managed version:

___

___

___

___

What it cost me. What it produced:

Day 9 — One moment today where the old pattern won. What happened, and what will I do differently:

Day 10 — Did I make a correction today — go back and correct something I said or omitted? What was it?

Day 11 — What is the hardest truth I am still avoiding saying? Why today?

Day 12 — How is my self-respect today compared to Day 1? What has changed, even slightly?

Day 13 — Did I contact my accountability partner this week? What did I tell them?

What did they reflect back?

Day 14 — End of Week Two. What is getting easier? What is still hard?

Week Three: Depth

This week goes deeper. Beyond the surface behavior — into the interior life. What are you feeling that you have not been saying? Where is the gap between your emotional reality and what you are presenting to the people around you?

Day 15 — What is one true thing about how I am doing emotionally that I have not told anyone?

Day 16 — What does my marriage actually need from me right now, beyond honesty about the deception? What kind of presence, attention, or truth?

Day 17 — What lie am I still telling myself — about why things are the way they are, about who is responsible, about what is possible?

Day 18 — Who have I been most honest with this week? Who have I been least honest with? Why the difference?

Day 19 — Read your Truth Declaration. Does it still feel true? What, if anything, needs to be added or revised?

Day 20 — What is the thing I am most afraid my wife will never forgive? Can I accept that possibility and continue choosing honesty anyway?

Day 21 — End of Week Three. What does the man you are becoming feel like from the inside? Describe it.

Week Four: Integration

The final week is about consolidation — making the new behavior feel less like effort and more like identity. You are not performing honesty anymore. You are practicing becoming someone for whom honesty is simply who you are.

Day 22 — Where did honesty feel natural today — not effortful, just the obvious thing?

Day 23 — What has changed in the quality of a relationship in your life — any relationship — as a result of greater honesty over these past weeks?

Day 24 — Where am I still managing? What is the last holdout — the place where the old pattern is most persistent?

Day 25 — What do I need to say that I still have not said? To whom? What is one concrete step toward saying it?

____

____

____

Day 26 — How is the relationship between my self-image and my actual behavior today, compared to Day 1?

____

____

____

Day 27 — What would the man I am becoming do today in the situation I am most tempted to manage?

____

____

____

Day 28 — Write a letter to the man you were at the beginning of this book. Tell him what you know now that he did not.

____

____

____

Day 29 — What accountability structure will I put in place to continue this work beyond these thirty days?

____

____

____

Day 30 — End of the Challenge. What is different? Not what do you hope is different. What is actually different, in your behavior, your interior life, your relationships? Write it plainly.

A FINAL NOTE

If you completed this workbook honestly — not perfectly, not without struggling, but honestly — then you have done something most men in your situation never do. You have turned toward the hardest thing instead of away from it. You have put the truth on paper and looked at it. You have made commitments to yourself in writing and held yourself accountable to them, at least in part, for thirty days.

That is not nothing. That is the beginning of something that can last.

The work does not end here. There is no point at which the commitment to honesty can be safely retired, no level of achievement at which you can stop paying attention and trust the old patterns not to resurface. This is a daily practice, in the same way that physical fitness is a daily practice — the gains are real and they compound over time, but they require continued investment.

What changes is the effort. In the beginning, honesty costs you enormously — every honest response is a conscious decision made against the grain of years of opposite behavior. Over time, with consistent practice, the grain reverses. Honesty becomes the easier path, the more natural one, the one that requires less effort than the managed version. That reversal does not happen in thirty days. But thirty days is where it starts.

You started it. Keep going.

— The Coach

ABOUT THE AUTHOR

Vasani Pettiford is one of the nation's leading voices in infidelity recovery and marriage restoration. As a bestselling author of over 18 books, a media personality, and co-founder of Couples Academy, he has dedicated his life to helping individuals and couples heal from the devastating impact of betrayal. For over two decades, Hasani has worked with high-profile clients—from professional athletes and entertainers to CEOs and everyday couples—guiding them through the most difficult relational crises with compassion, clarity, and conviction.

A master communicator, Hasani is a sought-after speaker and featured expert on networks such as NBC, BET, TLC, TV-One, TBN, and The CW. Through his transformative group intensives, private coaching, and online platforms, he has restored hope to thousands who once believed their marriages were beyond repair.

Hasani brings a unique blend of spiritual insight, psychological understanding, and practical tools to the work of infidelity recovery. His signature programs—Last Chance Weekend, Private Marriage Intensives, and the Moving Forward Program—have earned national recognition for their effectiveness in saving marriages on the brink of divorce.

When he's not coaching couples, hosting his popular podcast, or speaking on stages across the globe, Hasani enjoys spending time with his wife, Danielle, and their four children. Together, they are living examples of love restored and purpose reclaimed.

To learn more, connect with Hasani and explore Couples Academy's resources, visit: **www.couplesacademy.org**

www.ingramcontent.com/pod-product-compliance
Lightning Source LLC
LaVergne TN
LVHW010946110826
845149LV00015B/3232